ESTATE MANAGEMENT AND SYMPOSIUM

XENOPHON WAS born in the early 420s BCE to a wealthy Athenian family. He associated in his youth with the philosopher Socrates. In 401 BCE, three years after Athens's defeat in the Peloponnesian War, he accepted an invitation to serve with a mercenary army (the famous Ten Thousand) raised by Cyrus, brother of the king of Persia. Cyrus led his army in an unsuccessful attack on his brother. After Cyrus' death, Xenophon was one of the leaders of the Ten Thousand in their retreat to the sea. He was later exiled from Athens and settled by the Spartans in the Peloponnese. It was there that he started writing the extraordinarily wide variety of works for which he is now famous: a didactic historical fiction (the *Cyropaedia*), a contemporary history of Greece (the *Hellenica*), as well as Socratic dialogues and treatises on economics, hunting, horsemanship, and the Spartan constitution. His most famous work is *The Expedition of Cyrus*, his account of the march of the Ten Thousand. He died in the late 350s BCE.

ANTHONY VERITY was Master of Dulwich College before his retirement. His previous translations include Theocritus, *The Idylls* (2002), Pindar, *The Complete Odes* (2007), and Homer, *The Iliad* (2011) and *The Odyssey* (2018).

EMILY BARAGWANATH is Associate Professor in the Classics Department at the University of North Carolina at Chapel Hill. Her publications include *Motivation and Narrative in Herodotus* (2008), articles on the literary techniques employed by the Greek historians, and the co-edited volumes *Myth, Truth, and Narrative in Herodotus* (2012) and *Clio and Thalia: Attic Comedy and Historiography* (*Histos* Supplement 2017). At present she is writing a monograph on Xenophon's representation of women.

OXFORD WORLD'S CLASSICS

*For over 100 years Oxford World's Classics have brought
readers closer to the world's great literature. Now with over 700
titles—from the 4,000-year-old myths of Mesopotamia to the
twentieth century's greatest novels—the series makes available
lesser-known as well as celebrated writing.*

*The pocket-sized hardbacks of the early years contained
introductions by Virginia Woolf, T. S. Eliot, Graham Greene,
and other literary figures which enriched the experience of reading.
Today the series is recognized for its fine scholarship and
reliability in texts that span world literature, drama and poetry,
religion, philosophy, and politics. Each edition includes perceptive
commentary and essential background information to meet the
changing needs of readers.*

OXFORD WORLD'S CLASSICS

XENOPHON

Estate Management
and
Symposium

Translated by
ANTHONY VERITY

With an Introduction and Notes by
EMILY BARAGWANATH

OXFORD
UNIVERSITY PRESS

OXFORD
UNIVERSITY PRESS

Great Clarendon Street, Oxford, OX2 6DP,
United Kingdom

Oxford University Press is a department of the University of Oxford.
It furthers the University's objective of excellence in research, scholarship,
and education by publishing worldwide. Oxford is a registered trade mark of
Oxford University Press in the UK and in certain other countries

First published as an Oxford World's Classics paperback 2022

Impression: 1

Published in the United States of America by Oxford University Press
198 Madison Avenue, New York, NY 10016, United States of America

British Library Cataloguing in Publication Data
Data available

Library of Congress Control Number: 2022931923

ISBN 978-0-19-882351-3

Printed and bound in Great Britain by
Clays Ltd, Elcograf S.p.A.

I am grateful to my Chapel Hill colleagues Sharon James and the late Philip Stadter for their helpful comments on a draft of this Introduction. For Philip Stadter.
E.B.

CONTENTS

INTRODUCTION

Xenophon's Life, Times, and Works

XENOPHON was born in Athens in the last third of the fifth century BCE. Antiquity knew him in the first place as a philosopher. Making Xenophon the subject of one of his *Lives of the Philosophers*, the ancient biographer Diogenes Laertius described his first encounter with the individual who would most profoundly influence his life and his literary output:

> The story goes that Socrates met Xenophon in a narrow street, and that [Socrates] stretched out his staff to bar the way, and inquired where every kind of food was sold. Upon receiving his answer, he put another question, 'And where do human beings become good and honourable [*kaloi kagathoi*]?' Xenophon was at a loss; 'Follow me then,' said Socrates, 'and learn'. From that time on he was a student of Socrates. He was the first to note down and publish the conversation of Socrates . . . (2.48)

While doubtless apocryphal, the anecdote captures essential aspects of Xenophon's Socrates, and of Xenophon's preoccupations more generally. The first question, about food, ascribes to Socrates a topic that is real-world, accessible, egalitarian: this basic human need over-rides social distinctions. Xenophon in his literary works writes lucidly and accessibly about everyday topics of fundamental importance. He returns time and again to analogies that are familiar and real for his readers: and his expression of ideas is all the more effective for this. Xenophon's recording of Socrates' assumption in his second question that 'human beings' (*anthrōpoi*) have the potential to become *kaloi kagathoi*—'good and honourable'—captures Xenophon's interest in and transformation of the concept of 'gentlemanliness'. He sidelines its traditional class connotations in applying it with purely moral reference to people of both genders and across social statuses, as illustrated in the works translated in this volume.

Xenophon's are the only Socratic dialogues aside from Plato's that survive in full. A Socratic dialogue is a literary work that depicts Socrates in conversation with others. The genre of *logoi Sōkratikoi*, or Socratic literature, is probably fictional in essence: what we have are creative soundings, in which an author uses Socrates as the vehicle for exploring his own ideas and preoccupations, albeit anchored to specific historical moments, and peopled with historical individuals. Xenophon plays with this issue of historicity in having the narrator claim to have been an eyewitness to the symposium that is described in one of the works included in this volume: 'I should like to describe the company I was in when I came to this conclusion' (*Symposium* I.1). Attentive readers will realize that Xenophon the author was a child at the time; he cannot have been present.

Xenophon was not in Athens for Socrates' trial before an Athenian democratic jury court in 399 BCE, the guilty verdict, and his execution—events that cast a dark shadow over the end of the fifth century, and profoundly shaped the outlooks of all those of Socrates' circle. Xenophon had already left to join the Ten Thousand Greek mercenaries who fought alongside the Persian prince Cyrus in his attempt to usurp the throne from his brother, Artaxerxes. Xenophon had discussed this venture with Socrates, who correctly augured that his friendship with Cyrus might create problems for Xenophon in relation to the Athenians (*Anab.* 3.1.5). Xenophon accepted the philosopher's advice to consult the Oracle at Delphi about the expedition but botched the consultation by failing to ask the right preliminary question: he asked how best to go, not whether to go at all. Socrates chided him but advised that he must now carry out all the god's instructions (*Anab.* 3.5.7).

Xenophon's gripping autobiographical account of the expedition, *Anabasis* (or *The March Up-Country*), narrates the long journey he took inland in support of Cyrus, the death of Cyrus at the battle of Cunaxa (401 BCE), the Persians' treacherous assassination of the leaders of the Greek army, Xenophon putting himself forward to command (*Anab.* 3.1), and his crucial role in leading the remnants of the mercenary force from the heart of the Persian empire back to the shores of Greece. His self-portrait is one of a pious, virtuous individual, who makes mistakes but learns from them, and against all odds inspires a sense of unity and higher aspiration in the disparate army he leads, in the face not only of external dangers but of the men's own self-serving motivations. Afterwards, exiled from Athens as predicted by Socrates (the reason for the decree is however debated), Xenophon was settled by the Spartans, presumably thanks to his close relationship with and military service for King Agesilaus, on an idyllic estate in the Peloponnese (*Anab.* 5.4.7–13), where he seems to have spent some decades penning his considerable and highly eclectic literary output. Besides the Socratic dialogues and *Anabasis*, he wrote a history of Greece, a historical novel about the upbringing and career of Cyrus the Great, technical treatises on hunting and horsemanship, and more. When the Spartans lost the battle of Leuctra in 371 BCE, they lost their control of the Peloponnese, including Scillus. Xenophon fled to Corinth with his sons, and perhaps spent his last years there.

The twin factors of Socrates' influence, and the experience of the trials and tribulations involved in leading the mercenary army, were key in shaping Xenophon's profound interest, evident right across his literary oeuvre, in human character and relationships. He was especially drawn to the topic of ideal leadership: the capacity or lack thereof of human beings—whether they be philosophers, military commanders, kings, or indeed housewives, courtesans, or slaves—to lead and influence other human beings in enlightened fashion, and in a way that contributes to a mutual good. Ideal leadership for Xenophon has much in common with friendship; the good leader is also a friend to those he leads. For Xenophon, the capacity to be a good leader and friend sits high among measures of a person's virtue.

Socrates was influential in the developing contemporary interest in questions of morality and ethics—questions that animated Greek literature and thought from its very beginning, but were given new emphasis, and approached more systematically, at this time. One senses too that, within the turbulent first decades of the fourth century BCE, ethical ties and friendship were felt best to supply both meaning and security to life. Hence, perhaps, the move evident in the writings of Xenophon to focus more insistently on questions of character and morality.

The Works Included in this Edition

This volume presents Xenophon's two literary works that are concerned with Athenian private life. *Estate Management* (*Oeconomicus*) describes Socrates conversing on the topic of successful management of one's *oikos* (household, estate). The focus is a well-to-do Athenian household, which proves a testing ground for the moral qualities or 'gentlemanliness' of the male head of household, but also a space in which the role and agency of women turn out to be key. *Symposium* shifts to the male space of the men's quarters of the private home, to describe an evening of conversation and entertainment at the house of an Athenian plutocrat. Far from being simply a light-hearted affair, the conversation probes timeless questions regarding wisdom, love, and female capacity, and over it looms the deadly serious matter of Socrates' trial and death.

Both works are rich sources for Athenian social history of the Classical period. *Estate Management* in particular offers insights on the role and status of women in Ancient Athens. Xenophon does not, however, passively reflect the social realities he saw around him or supply snapshots of historical actuality. Both are Socratic dialogues, and first and foremost literary creations that reveal Xenophon as a skilled literary artist, an innovative thinker, and—far from merely reflecting the conventional thinking of the world around him—as indicating directions in which one might aspire to change that world. Their dialogic character complicates interpretation, but I shall argue that both works indicate that exemplary moral qualities may be displayed even by women and slaves, whose lesser moral and intellectual standing was taken for granted in contemporary Athens. This picture of a very broad basis of human capacity for virtue is radical. It can speak to our own times.

Estate Management

In this work Socrates converses with the unsuccessful Athenian householder Critobulus. Within that conversation, reported in direct discourse, is nested an earlier conversation Socrates had with the exemplary householder Ischomachus, and nested within that conversation are still others, including that of Ischomachus and his wife.

THE *OIKOS* AND ITS IMPORTANCE

The *oikos*—'estate', 'household', or 'family'—embraced one's house, family, slaves,[1] and animals, and the broader estate (several non-adjacent farms or fields in Ischomachus' case) and everything it produced and

---

[1] Slavery was an essential institution of Greek societies. It was not structured and justified by race (as in the United States), though most slaves were foreigners. The closest we find to someone imagining a world without it is Xenophon's Socrates' invitation to his interlocutor to agree that enslaving other people is in general unjust (*Mem.* 4.2.14). Xenophon also exposes slavery's violence (as when he has Ischomachus implicitly admit that his enslaved women do not want him forcing sex on them (X.12)).

consumed. In this work the interest of Socrates (ventriloquized by Xenophon) in the science of *oikonomia* ('household/estate management') and his concern to define its scope and function is a first indication of the topic's importance. Socrates contextualizes his inquiry into *oikos* management within his broader inquiry as to who are 'the most knowledgeable in the city' (II.16), an inquiry stimulated by his surprising discovery that the same activity makes some people poor, others extremely rich (II.17). The second indication is the work's sheer length: the extensive account of his household provided by the ideal Athenian gentleman Ischomachus, at times taken to indicate a pedantic husband's penchant for micro-management, finds a parallel in Xenophon's thorough treatment of other important topics (for instance, the detailed account in *Education of Cyrus* of the reforms of the famed Persian king).

Xenophon employs a sustained strategy of presenting matters of estate management as equally important to civic administration, politics, and warfare. Socrates invokes Cyrus the Great: 'They say that he considers farming and warfare to be among the most glorious and essential professions there are, and consequently devotes vigorous attention to both' (IV.4). Xenophon figures successful household management and its requisite skills in terms of *erga* (deeds, works, achievements) that are worthy of record and memory, so putting it on a par with the great deeds judged worthy of inclusion in histories. One such achievement of household management that is 'worth looking into' is how 'in some households nearly all [slaves] are held in chains and yet keep running away, whereas in others they have some freedom and are willing to work and remain at their stations' (III.4). Socrates' interlocutor Critobulus has been known to wake at the crack of dawn and walk miles to see a comedy, trying to persuade Socrates to join him; 'but you have never yet invited me to watch a performance [*ergon*] like the one I mentioned'—the real-life example of the willing slaves (III.7). So Xenophon intimates that this genre concerned with everyday life is more valuable than Athens's beloved dramatic productions. Socrates would more gladly hear about Ischomachus' training of his wife 'than a description of even the most brilliant athletic contest or horse race!' (VII.9) The thrill he anticipates rivals that of the sporting events celebrated in praise poetry.

The attention paid to the domestic sphere accords with Xenophon's broader approach. Elsewhere he presents *oikoi* as standing not in opposition to the *polis* (city state), but as its very building-blocks

(*Mem.* 3.6.14). The examination of the *oikos* as foundation of the wealth of the individual and of the individual family complements his consideration elsewhere (in *Poroi*, or *Ways and Means*) of Athenian civic finances, the financial foundation of the community of *oikoi*. The two spheres, public and private, are also complementary in that for Xenophon the very same human relational dynamics, and the similar transferable skills, cut across spheres. The all-important capacity to govern other people is (as Ischomachus puts it) 'common to every activity, be it farming, politics, estate management, or warfare' (XXI.2; Xenophon attributes similar remarks to Socrates, as at *Memorabilia* 3.4.12). In *Estate Management* the wife, housekeeper, foremen, and slaves all demonstrate (or are said to have the potential to demonstrate) the skills required by commanders or civic administrators.

The attention to the *oikos* is also a symptom of Xenophon's holistic approach. His anthropological interests as they surface across his literary works span the full swathe of humanity: Greeks and non-Greeks, Athenians and Spartans, commanders and common soldiers, men and women, free and slave. The depictions range across settings overseas, within Greek cities, and—in *Estate Management*—within the house; and encompass past and present. The categories of humankind are invoked in ways that suggest the value he places on the perspectives of different stripes of humanity. In this work he depicts Socrates' desire to encounter Ischomachus as piqued by the fact of hearing him referred to as a model gentleman 'universally . . . in the opinion of women as well as men, foreigners as well as citizens' (*Oec.* VI.17). Socrates invokes the frustration felt by slaves, as well as their owners, at their incapacity swiftly to find what they seek in the house (III.2); and the perspectives of (in this order) slaves, wives, and children, as well as friends (at V.10), as proof of the delight that farming gives.

THE ROLE OF WOMEN

In writing a lengthy treatise devoted to household management, Xenophon displayed an interest remarkable for his time. Not since Homer's *Odyssey* had there appeared such an extended reflection on the *oikos* and the role and agency of women within it. Penelope may be understood as an exemplary wife, and as Odysseus' true companion and equal. She is an exception: Homer's time and the centuries that follow offer few depictions of wives, and very few indeed that are readable as positive appraisals. In Hesiod's poem the wife is an economic burden and existential threat to the *oikos* her husband has worked so hard to establish. The biting satire on women penned by Semonides, another poet of the archaic age (seventh century BCE), draws connections in vice between women and an extended catalogue of animals; a single, virtuous bee-woman makes an appearance only at the very end. (To this lone paragon Xenophon in *Estate Management* makes reference, transforming the image into one of the *queen* bee, a model of wifely leadership, industry, and the just management of people (VII.32–4).)

In the Classical Athenian democracy, women were relegated to second-class status, and considered to be intellectually and morally infirm. The women who mattered—citizen women,[2] charged with bearing citizen sons—were to be seen, heard, and spoken of as little as possible. Thucydides' Pericles, in his funeral oration early in the Peloponnesian War, only reluctantly offered any words of consolation and advice to Athens' grieving female relatives:

If I must say anything about female virtue, to those who will now be in widowhood, I will signal everything in a short exhortation: great will be your reputation if you don't fall short of your nature, and greatest will be hers who is least talked about among men, whether for praise or blame. (2.45.2)

Thucydides himself follows this paradoxical advice—according to which women's only fame should be not to have any fame at all—in excising them almost completely from his history.

Xenophon's *Estate Management* goes directly against the grain of such attitudes. The work makes the case that the *oikos* is crucial to the functioning of society, that women's role within it is key, that women are eminently capable of rational thought and articulate speech and conducting mutually beneficial relationships; and that they, like men, are licensed to win praise for this.

Estate Management underscores the particular value within the domestic sphere of female work and agency. Socrates asks failing householder Critobulus:

'we're all friends here, and so you must tell us the truth; is there anyone to whom you entrust more matters of importance than to your wife?' 'No

---

[2] Free women, with Athenian citizen parents, as opposed to foreigners or slaves.

one.' 'Is there anyone with whom you talk less than with your wife?' 'No one—or not many, at any rate.' (III.12)

The exemplary (if amusingly prolix) gentleman Ischomachus, on the other hand, indicates that he has leisure to pursue his other social and civic obligations precisely because his wife is perfectly capable of running the house. Time and again he draws attention to the importance of her role. When Socrates broaches the topic that forms the crux of the work, in asking how he earned the sobriquet 'gentleman' (since he clearly does not spend his time indoors), Ischomachus directly invokes his wife: he does not live indoors, since 'my wife is more than capable of managing our domestic affairs on her own' (VII.3). Socrates asks how this happy situation came to be. The account Ischomachus provides apparently receives his endorsement: he reports it to Critobulus (in the temporally posterior conversation that opens the work) in advising him on household management.

Initially Ischomachus' young bride (14 years old (VII.5)—around half the age of her husband) conformed wholly to normative Athenian ideals: she came to him having 'lived under strict supervision, which meant that she saw, heard, and spoke as little as possible', and well schooled in controlling her appetite (VII.5–6). He set about training her, a process that transformed her into something quite beyond expectations, as Ischomachus wittily signals: he began questioning her 'as soon as she was tamed and sufficiently domesticated—to carry on a conversation ("to engage in dialogue", *dialegesthai*)'; and his very first reported word to her urges her (in the imperative) to 'Speak' (VII.10). The notion of the young bride being tamed *to speak* upends the conventional expectations brought to mind by the taming metaphor. Speech (*logos*) for the Greeks, which covers the spectrum from 'word' to 'reason', is the quintessential expression of human rationality. *Dialegein*—'to engage in dialogue'—is the central plank of Socratic intellectual endeavour.

Ischomachus repeatedly invokes his wife's intellectual capacity and powers of judgement, employing first-person plurals to describe the deliberations they will undertake together (as about the education of their future children (VII.12)) and their co-teaching of the housekeeper, not only in the practical aspects of her role but in such moral virtues as self-control, loyalty (IX.12), and justice (IX.13). She gradually gains confidence, asks questions of her own, and even questions some of her husband's assumptions. Once Ischomachus was charged (on what crime is unspecified) and found guilty—and (it turns out) the judge was his wife, who holds him to high standards of truth-telling (XI.25). Frequently Ischomachus expresses her value through such metaphors drawn from the Athenian civic sphere as judge/juror, nomophylax (guardian of laws), phrourarch (garrison commander), or even the boule (Council) in its role of inspecting the cavalry (IX.15). Arguably these encapsulate the way he, an Athenian male, envisages his wife's role, and they help his (male) listeners, and of course Xenophon's readers, conceptualize it as well. And yet, far from only comparing his wife to men, Xenophon has Ischomachus underscore the distinctly feminine qualities that make women the natural carers of children and stewards of the domestic domain.

Ischomachus observes that men and women preside over different spheres: the outside and inside respectively. Each is superior to the other in his or her respective sphere, their natural qualities equipping them to perform their respective roles. The beneficial complementarity of male and female spheres is divinely ordained. The god designed men to be better able to bear cold, heat, travel, and military service, and so undertake outdoor activities. In women he instilled greater love of infants, and a timidity that made for a better guardian of the household goods. But in their moral capacity men and women are equal:

Since both have also to give and take, he apportioned memory and concern [*epimeleia*] even-handedly to both, so that you could not differentiate between male and female as to who has the greater part of these qualities. Self-control [*enkrateia*] too the god has distributed impartially to both, and has determined that whichever of them, man or woman, shows greater aptitude in this shall enjoy more of the benefit which flows from it. (VII.22–7)

These are the qualities needed to achieve successful human relationships, which for Xenophon rely above all on one's understanding of reciprocity: of how 'to give and take'.

When his wife doubts that her indoor tasks could be as valuable as his outdoor duties, Ischomachus insists that each activity would be ridiculous and futile in the absence of the other (VII.39–40). Among her highlighted responsibilities is her financial agency in the *oikos*, including her accountancy role in overseeing all the income. Beyond illuminating the sheer quantity of labour she undertakes, Ischomachus insists upon the moral capacities required by the work of *oikos* management: her activities as much as her husband's 'demand work and care' (VII.22). When she doubts how helpful she can be, since her mother taught her only self-control (*sōphrosunē* (VII.14)), Ischomachus says that he too learned this from his father, and, remarkably, he defines it as a quality shared by men and women and expressed in the good management of the household: keeping the property in good shape and adding to it by honest means (VII.15). Female *sōphrosunē* was traditionally understood to be reflected rather in reticence and chastity. His wife is not only self-controlled herself; she is tasked with judging *sōphrosunē* in others: charged with rewarding self-disciplined and helpful slaves, and punishing the lazy (VII.42). As for the virtue of obedience, despite its importance elsewhere to the military man Xenophon, it is here largely downplayed (though see X.1). He is perhaps purposefully pushing back against conventional conceptions of women that assumed the need for them to be controlled and contained. Instead, he highlights female agency and authority. What keep a woman indoors are her considerable responsibilities.

Responding to Ischomachus' counsel to uphold order (a cardinal virtue for Xenophon), she demonstrates an intuitive grasp of its value: her husband has fallen short in his judgement if he thinks it bothersome for her to care for her own property. ' "For just as it seems more natural," she said, "for a sensible [*sōphrōn*] woman to care for her children than to neglect them, so such a person will find it more satisfying to look after [*epimeleisthai*] her possessions than to neglect them, inasmuch as they belong to her" ' (IX.19). Here she picks up on his vocabulary of attentiveness (*epimeleia*), extending the idea of women's natural care for children to cover household possessions as well. At this Socrates remarks, 'Well, I declare, Ischomachus, you're telling me your wife thinks like a man!' (X.1). This—or, rather, that men and women think in the same way—is exactly what Ischomachus has been trying to prove.

The wife's moral qualities (especially *enkrateia*, *sōphrosunē*, and *epimeleia*) are those of all Xenophon's excellent leaders. The idea of the wife as effective leader within the household is conveyed most strikingly in the image of the queen bee, which stems not from contemporary scientific knowledge (which assumed a male, king bee), but from the metaphor Xenophon takes care to construct. The analogy encapsulates brilliantly her leadership role overseeing and forging relationships with the members of the household, whom she instructs in their activities; how she knows, receives, and safeguards everything brought in; and how she then 'allots each bee its fair (or "just") share' (VII.33). This highlights both her industriousness and the moral dimension of her role.

When Ischomachus suggests that the duty to care for sick slaves may seem to her rather thankless (VII.37), she vehemently counters with what she sees as the delight of that task, revealing an intuitive understanding—transcending his—of the positive reciprocal relationship that may be forged from her care (VII.37), and of the fact that slaves share in this relationship economy as well (a truth demonstrated elsewhere in *Estate Management*). Her focus more on the slaves' perceptions than on material outcomes makes clear that she understands the value of positive relationships. Here as elsewhere in Xenophon, when it comes to relationships and the ethics of care we get a sense of a woman's particular sensibilities and natural expertise. Again, her role as companion and partner to her husband is given more emphasis than her role (the usual focus of Greek attitudes) as producer of children.

The wife may even prove morally superior to her husband. Her greatest pleasure, Ischomachus remarks, 'will be if you are seen to be better than me, and can make me your servant' (VII.42). As she grows older, rather than losing respect, she will win honour by proving a better partner to Ischomachus and guardian for the children of their estate (VII.42). He tells her: 'It is not because of youthful attractiveness that what is good and beautiful [*ta . . . kala te k'agatha*] multiplies in human lives, but through the exercise of virtues' (VII.43). The expression invokes and connects to the discussion of the wife the very ideal of gentlemanliness.

Though initially described as the training of a wife, the account reveals the spouses' shared agency in the process, as he teaches her to the best of his ability, and she learns to the best of hers. The successful outcome depends on her possession of key moral virtues and a keen intelligence. Ischomachus is so long-winded in detailing his wife's role in the household that Socrates has to prompt him to turn to describing his own; and Socrates assures him that *both* husband and wife deserve to win much praise (XI.1).

Is this picture undermined by the extratextual history? How Ischomachus' wife Chrysilla, after his death, went on to have a scandalous relationship with her son-in-law Callias (*Andocides* 1; the same

Callias appears in Xenophon's *Symposium*)? Some have thought so. And yet Xenophon often highlights ideals against a backdrop of failure. The final book of *The Education of Cyrus* charts the dissolution, after his death, of Cyrus' ideal government. Rather than undermining the content of the work, the effect may be destabilizing: it may oblige readers to contemplate the challenge of translating ideals into reality, and of sustaining virtue over time. Cyrus' achievement may be burnished, not undone, by how Persia slides into disorder afterwards. Similarly, the sordid future of Ischomachus' household, if Xenophon knew and expected his readers to know about it, throws into sharper relief the ideal that for some time had been realized. The eventual failure perhaps also contributes to the defence of Socrates, by underscoring the dynamic quality of human character: it can improve, but if one neglects to practise virtue, it will deteriorate. In this way, once Socrates' notorious students Alcibiades and Critias were no longer subject to his beneficial influence, they went off the rails (as Xenophon tells us explicitly at *Mem.* 1.2.21–8). Their toxic actions surely helped bring Socrates to trial. The implicit foil of Callias and his household also reinforces several of the dialogue's themes that have a bearing on female agency: the responsibility of husbands to teach their wives and so establish productive partnerships in which the women understand their responsibilities and have a sense of their higher purpose; the importance of *epimeleia* (attention, care)—about which the profligate dilettante Callias had no clue; the theme of exemplarity as unconnected to high birth (Callias was of the bluest of blue blood).

REDEFINING *KALOKAGATHIA* (GENTLEMANLINESS, EXEMPLARITY)

Estate Management startlingly destabilizes key assumptions of traditional Greek aristocratic ideology about *kalokagathia*—'gentlemanliness', literally 'beauty and (moral) goodness'. Conventionally these qualities were regarded as an almost automatic concomitant of wealth and social position. Early on it is established that, since wealth is only what is useful, land itself (typical upper-class economic reserve) is not always wealth, as in the case of owners who have knowledge and means to enlarge their estates, but fail to do so through unwillingness to work (I.16). These include even the highest born, when ruled by 'masters' such as laziness, moral infirmity, and negligence (I.18). Similarly, in this metaphorical sense, slaves are those who impoverish their estates because of the masters—gluttony, lechery, drunkenness, and costly and senseless ambitions (I.21). Socrates makes the slavery metaphor vivid with his remark that one must fight for one's freedom against such masters 'as hard as against those who are attempting to enslave us by force of arms' (I.23), since they do constant outrage to our bodies, souls, and *oikoi*. The ensuing conversation exposes the fact that Critobulus—gentleman though he initially seemed, a well-heeled individual called on by the city to fund triremes and dramatic competitions—risks becoming a pauper (II.7–9). This discussion of slavery is the first in a sustained manoeuvre whereby the dialogue over-throws traditional aristocratic conceptions to reveal a hierarchy that depends almost exclusively upon virtue. Thereby unveiled is a topsy-turvy world. The very term *kalos kagathos*—the traditional epithet for a gentleman of high birth—is divorced from its traditional connections to socioeconomic status when Ischomachus remarks of his slaves:

If . . . I observe men who are disposed to behave honestly not only because of the advantages this gives them but also because they are anxious for my praise, I treat them as free men, enriching them and even honouring them as gentlemen [*kaloi kagathoi*]. (XIV.9)

The moral inflection of the term *kaloi kagathoi* in this context is unmistakable. (See also *Memorabilia* 1.1.16.)

Elsewhere, too, we see that slaves can possess the qualities of free men and of masters (and vice versa), including specifically the cap-acity to govern others. The slave foreman is capable of being trained to manage (rule, govern) other people (XIII.4). Socrates underscores the significance of this: 'Anyone who can train people to be capable of governing others can clearly also train them to exercise mastery, and if he can make men fit to be masters he can also make them fit to be kings' (XIII.5). Kingliness itself is, then, available to people right across the social spectrum. The same quality is available across gen-ders: the wife is likened both to a queen (IX.15) and a queen bee (VII.32–3), while the slave housekeeper possesses the moral capacity (IX.11–12) that for Xenophon allows one both to sustain reciprocal relationships and where necessary to govern others.

Much as the concept of 'gentleman' comes to embrace a far wider spectrum of people than simply the well-born, so nobility itself is depicted as wholly accessible: it is especially since farming is the easiest art to learn that (Ischomachus remarks) 'it must surely be something noble [*gennaion*]' (XV.4). Along with its accessibility are farming's qualities of superlative helpfulness and sweetness (XV.4, cf. 5). The famous image of Xenophon as 'Attic Bee' perhaps combines with the idea of the sweetness and clarity of his prose style an idea of accessibility: for as well as making honey, the bee is prevalent in Athens, and flits freely, alighting upon flowers of all description.

Xenophon's generous conception of where virtue can lie helps explain how it is that such different individuals as Socrates and Ischomachus can both be regarded as exemplary. They may be alternative positive models (as scholar Louis-André Dorion argues; David Johnson counters that Ischomachus is at best a limited model). Barefoot, impoverished Socrates is a less accessible model for most Athenian householders to aspire to than the well-to-do Ischomachus with his more conventional mode of life. The penniless Socrates is superlatively helpful to others, as *Memorabilia* demonstrates in sustained fashion. At times this helpfulness takes the form, for instance, of revealing to individuals the true worth of their various occupations. In *Estate Management* he assists Critobulus with practical life advice that among other things will help him improve his financial situation. Material prosperity in *Estate Management* is seen in terms of its value to others: Ischomachus explains to Socrates that he desires to make money so as to be in a position to make lavish offerings to the gods, to help a friend in need, and to contribute to the city's embellishment (XI.10): purely honourable motivations. Xenophon lauds those who help their fellow human beings in any capacity.

TEACHING AND LEARNING

Farming exemplifies the work's profoundly democratic guiding idea: that anyone can learn. So it is that the earth reveals clearly, to anyone who pays attention, the principles of agriculture. Indeed, despite not being a farmer, Socrates finds he already understands the essentials of farming. He tells Ischomachus:

Is it that questioning, then, is a kind of teaching? The fact is, I have just seen through your method of questioning me step by step: you lead me through what I know, and then mention something similar to it, and persuade me that I know things that I thought I didn't. (XIX.15)

Rather than pulling the rug out from under him (as often in the case of the Platonic Socrates), the questioning process exposes knowledge that the dialogue partner already possesses. In this instance it reveals that even Socrates—notoriously deficient in skills of estate management—possesses knowledge precisely in this area. That the principles of farming are readily graspable does not undercut their importance.

The explicit remarks on pedagogy—on how most effectively to convey information (how to make it clearer and more impactful, as at XVII.15)—highlight the premium set on clarity and accessibility. Ischomachus is an effective teacher, his wife an excellent pupil (e.g. X.13). Ischomachus praises the simplicity and clarity with which the land communicates truths (e.g. XX.13–14); and this is a model of communication to which Xenophon himself (to judge by the clarity of his prose) evidently subscribes.

The dialogue also illustrates the reversibility of teaching direction: the follower turns out to possess the knowledge of a leader: Socrates is teacher vis-à-vis Critobulus, but learner vis-à-vis Ischomachus. And it turns out that the wife, just like Socrates, already possesses a great deal of knowledge, and potentially can even teach her husband. A similar principle of reversibility applies to Xenophon's ideas about leadership: good leaders or rulers are themselves in various ways subject to rule, above all, rule of themselves or self-control.

The crucial art of farming the land is accessible to all, and, by means of it, everyone has the potential to demonstrate virtue.

THE UNDERESTIMATION OF XENOPHON

In summary, *Estate Management* presents a remarkable picture indeed. Yet modern scholarship has been oddly dismissive, loath to accept the radical nature of the work's content. Why should that be?

One explanation is the long shadow cast by the influential political philosopher and classical scholar Leo Strauss. In expounding his theory, embraced by generations of American political scientists, that Xenophon's works do not mean what at first sight—from a careful, direct reading of the text—they seem to mean, he made *Estate Management* a central text. According to Strauss's conviction—one formed in the shadow of the rise of Nazism in Germany in the early years of the twentieth century (Strauss, of Jewish descent, left his homeland in the 1930s, never to live there again)—the philosopher stands in opposition to the city (the *polis*). He cannot speak openly, so communicates with his target group of elite readers through suggestion and innuendo. To understand Xenophon's true meaning one must therefore read between the lines with an eye above all for what is *not* said. Therefore, in *Estate Management*, contrary to all appearances, Socrates does not endorse the views of the gentleman and man of the city, Ischomachus: Socrates' reticence indicates that, far from agreeing with Ischomachus, he regards him as a babbling fool. Out with the bathwater of Ischomachus' advice went also, for instance, his percipient remarks on women.

Strauss's view of the philosopher standing in opposition to the city would also make unimaginable the wise man who is political and supports the city and its interests. Though crucial to Xenophon's depiction, it cannot envisage a political Socrates; yet *Memorabilia* portrays a Socrates deeply involved in the life of the city of Athens, interested in its citizens and the quality of its governance. Strauss's notion of the philosopher who hides his convictions from citizens in general also overlooks how Socrates exemplified the normal ancient Greek understanding of philosophy as a way of life. In Xenophon's depiction, Socrates' words and convictions were mirrored in his actions. More broadly, across his works Xenophon demonstrates the vital importance of the words of potential leaders matching their actions, and the appearance of virtue signalling the reality of virtue that lies beneath. Strauss's notion of reading Xenophon between the lines to extract a concealed message addressed to a narrow, elite circle also flies in the face of the style and character of Xenophon's works, and their at times explicit endorsement of openness, readability, and accessibility.

The very readability and accessibility of Xenophon point to another explanation for the failure to see him for the creative thinker he is. Xenophon promotes delight and sweetness in the reading experience. So it is that he softens the effect of ideas that might otherwise strike readers as too radical, whether by clothing them in conventional guises, or presenting them as rooted in traditional origins. The subversive arguments of *Estate Management*—those regarding gentlemanliness itself, and the moral capacity of women and slaves—are found on the lips of a most traditional gentleman, and one who has learned all he knows from his own father (XX.22). The novel propositions about gender are framed by the hallowed notion of the divine ordering of the cosmos. Farming, most traditional aristocratic occupation, is the model—but it opens up a conception of virtue as available to everyone.

Such strategies, aimed at the delight and the persuasion of the work's original readers, have had the effect of amplifying for modern readers its conservative hue.

There has also been simple unwillingness to acknowledge that Xenophon—or perhaps any individual of his gender, time, background, and experience—could pen such a work as Estate Management, or even think such thoughts. In line with more general assumptions held about Xenophon as backward- rather than forward-looking, as plodding and conventional rather than visionary, so too has he been assumed, in *Estate Management*, to be capable only of simply reflecting the world around him, rather than possessing the interest and imagination to envisage other ways that world *could* be. *Estate Management* has most often been read as a reflection of social realities, a convenient source to be mined by social-history textbooks, but hardly worthy of analysis in its own right. The (to modern sensibilities) exhaustive detail has, accordingly, been taken as faithfully rendering actuality, rather than as the rhetorical strategy it is: for the level of detail underscores the importance of the topic and shapes a picture to which it lends an impression of incontrovertibility, even as it may also characterize Ischomachus as comically verbose in his enthusiasm.

Again, Xenophon's efforts at clarity in both style and content, as in the recurrence of key ideas and the choice of simple, bold metaphors, have been taken to be the reflection of a limited mind, rather than opening up its content to a potentially quite wide and diverse audience. Even the remarkable depiction of Ischomachus' wife, while it has attracted much notice, has been disarmed by interpretations explaining it in terms of her assimilation to her husband, his concern for the domestic sphere interpreted as (male-chauvinist) micro-management and mansplaining. This tendency is evident even at the level of construal of the text and translation of the Greek, activities that naturally already involve interpretation: clear meanings have been distorted in a bid to make the text conform to scholarly assumptions about Xenophon's meaning.

But if, instead, we take the essay on its own terms, we must recognize that, far from cleaving to conventional perspectives, *Estate Management* airs unexpected viewpoints that prompt in readers deeper reflection and even shifts in attitude. The work's layers of surprise are connected to the presentation of revised perspectives, such as Socrates' alerting Critobulus to the wonder of how his perspective has shifted from regarding Socrates as impoverished, to recognizing in himself the true pauper (II.9). And it may be that in this Xenophon captures something of the instructional methods of the historical Socrates.

Symposium

From the family sphere of the *oikos*, domain of women and men, we turn to Xenophon's *Symposium* and the Athenian household's exclusively male quarters. Several themes connect to those of *Estate Management*. The essay also engages with Plato's *Symposium* in ways that illuminate notable points of divergence. The relative dating of the works is debated: Xenophon's Socrates' long speech near the end (ch. 8) responds explicitly to Plato's *Symposium* (written between 384 and 379 BCE: see Dover, *Plato Symposium*, 10), and so that part at least clearly postdates it. The sympotic intermingling of humour and seriousness charges the conversation with potentially destabilizing irony.

FROM GENTLEMANLINESS TO EXEMPLARITY

The subject matter of the work, so the opening sentence declares, is the activities, in their light-hearted moments, of 'men who are gentlemen' (*kaloi kagathoi*, 'noble and good'). The occasion is a horse race (an aristocratic pastime), to which glitzy plutocrat Callias has invited the beautiful young athletic victor he is courting (in the context of the typically aristocratic institution of male/male pederasty). For the evening Callias plans a celebratory dinner, or symposium (a 'drinking together', another characteristically aristocratic male recreation). This constellation of elements implicitly defines *kalokagathia* ('gentlemanliness', literally 'nobility/beauty and goodness') in conventional terms, as the attribute of men of the highest social status and significant wealth. The ensuing work contests such an assumption, however. As in *Estate Management* (above), Xenophon redefines *kalokagathia*, broadening its potential application so that the term and concept denote a quality of excellence (something like 'exemplarity') open to those of lower economic status, and even perhaps to women and slaves.

Callias encounters Socrates by chance and invites his group to join the party: men 'pure in their souls' will lend more glamour to the evening than his typical guests ('generals and cavalry commanders and ambitious place-seekers' (I.4)). Callias' wealth provides a foil to Socrates' poverty (to which Xenophon draws attention, unlike Plato in his *Symposium*), another guest argues that poverty is his most valuable possession, and several indicate that true riches reside elsewhere than in things material. Where Plato's essay was exclusionary, Xenophon's embraces people of various social statuses and of both genders. The slaves' performances are a particular focus. They punctuate and give structure to the dialogue. Partway through the evening Socrates observes that it would be shameful if the diners, too, 'didn't try, while we're here together, to give each other some benefit or pleasure' (III.2). The slave performers indeed supply the guests, and Xenophon's readers, not only with entertainment but also (as Socrates' mediating voice brings out) with serious food for thought.

Socrates confounds the conventional strict ideological demarcation in Classical Athens into separate categories of different statuses of women, citizen wives over against all others (the classic statement is Ps-Demosthenes, *Against Neaera* 59.122): he invokes the female slave acrobat's astonishing capacity as proof that the men should confidently teach their wives whatever they would have them learn (II.8). (Similarly at *Oec.* III.14 he cites the courtesan Aspasia as an authority on the training of citizen wives.) Antisthenes acidly counters that Socrates does not appear to have trained his own notoriously difficult wife. Socrates replies that he chose her for the very reason of her high-spiritedness: he desires to live among and deal with his fellow human beings (*anthrōpoi*), and 'if I can put up with her I shall have no difficulty in getting along with the rest of humankind [*anthrōpoi*]' (II.10). So he presents his wife as exemplary of all human beings, his marriage as the foundation and training ground for the relationships he develops with others. The comment is amusing and paradoxical, but also highlights the importance to Xenophon and his Socrates of relationships.

Socrates' interlocutor here, Antisthenes, is the Socratic famous for his dictum that 'virtue is the same for a man and a woman' (Diogenes Laertius, *Lives of the Philosophers* 6.12). The female performer, in confidently leaping through knives, demonstrates (so Socrates observes) that 'courage [*andreia*, lit. 'manliness'] too is something that can be taught' (II.12). (We might compare Socrates' remark at *Oec.* X.1 on the exemplary wife's 'manly intellect'.) Two of the diners comically amplify this serious point by proposing that Athens pay the slave master to display her to the Athenians to teach them courage in battle. The banter sustains the work's motif of the interrelation of the playful and the serious. Socrates' perplexing remark that the acrobat's performance 'is but one of many proofs that women's natural abilities are actually in no way inferior tó men's—except that they are deficient in judgement and physical strength' (II.9) is susceptible to divergent interpretations, depending on whether and how one reads the possible humour (as in Socrates' underscoring the parity of women's and men's nature only to indicate a major qualification ('except that . . .'), or in the collision of scripts of slave entertainer and citizen wife).

In any case, against the backdrop of the exclusively male space of the *andrōn* (men's quarters), the work highlights women and their value and draws attention to heterosexuality in the context of marriage. At times the conversation turns to the men's wives and imagines their perspectives—for instance, Niceratus' wife's approval should her spouse arrive home with onion breath (assurance of his faithfulness). The early scene of chaste homoeroticism (I.7–10) is answered in the sexually-explicit closing vision of heterosexual marital love: the slaves' mime of Dionysus and Ariadne, which prompts the premature conclusion of the gathering. At the racy floorshow the bachelors vow to marry, while the husbands—forgoing the usual final stage of a symposium, the rowdy kommos that often included sex with the hired entertainers—jump on their horses and race home 'to enjoy some wedded bliss' (IX.7).

RELATIONSHIPS

Philosophia is the love (*philia*) of wisdom (*sophia*). In the *Symposium*, as in his other more philosophical works (the Socratic essays, *Cyropaedia*, *Hiero*), we find Xenophon valuing *sophia* above all in the context of human connections (rather than in the abstract, as often in Plato). Xenophon places less emphasis on *sophia* than on capacity to conduct exemplary relationships—that is to say, capacity for *philia* (love in the sense of friendship), which for Xenophon can encompass most human relationships in their exemplary forms. One guest, Antisthenes, goes so far as to claim that justice—the relational virtue par excellence—is the quality most equivalent to general excellence (*kalokagathia*), since it is absolutely always a good thing. Not so wisdom (*sophia*) and courage, which can at times seem to harm one's friends and the city (III.4). (Xenophon's Socrates counters that thesis in the *Memorabilia*, equating 'justice and every other form of virtue' with *sophia* (3.9.5).)

The *Symposium* shows how positive human relationships may be conducive to intellectual and moral improvement. Most notably, Callias' love for Autolycus has the potential to stimulate him towards virtue (see below). We are given a first indication of the importance to the *Symposium* of relationships, and of the relational dimension of acquiring knowledge, in how the narrator frames the work's opening: he 'should like to describe the company (he) was in' when he realized the value of gentlemen's deeds even at play. For the Greeks it was an adage (found in Xenophon at *Symposium* 2.4, *Memorabilia* 1.2.20–1, cf. 1.4.1, 1.2.18–24: the example of Socrates) that the character of those whose company you keep directly influences your own: you learn good morals from spending time with the best people (who conventionally were equated with those of high class, the *aristoi*, 'the best'). Xenophon and his Socrates democratize the idea by indicating that one may learn valuable knowledge from people of all stripes and across the status spectrum (even the doubly-sidelined female slave). Elsewhere, especially in the conversations of *Memorabilia*, Xenophon presents Socrates as benefiting his community by showing all its members (including a prostitute: *Mem.* 3.11) the value to wider society of their particular understanding or expertise.

Xenophon presents wisdom and understanding, whether abstract or specialized, intellectual or more practical, as accessible to a broad base of humanity. (Cf. *Oec.* XI–XX in the context of farming, nature makes the most important knowledge accessible to all.) There is added value, then, in bringing together the contributions and divergent perspectives of many, as at this symposium, and acknowledging that wisdom is not the prerogative of Socrates alone. We hear the opinions of the other guests, but also the perspectives of the wives at home (as the men imagine them) (IV.8, VIII.3), and of the slaves charged to judge the beauty contest between Socrates and Critobulus (V.8–9). The vision is less hierarchical than Plato's, in whose *Symposium* Socrates' understanding trumps that of the other guests, including in how he alone has had access to and reports the (exclusive, divine) knowledge of the priestess Diotima. Her image of the path to understanding of universal beauty is a (tall and narrow) ladder (Plato, *Symposium* 211c).

In Ancient Greece one typically aristocratic and exclusive context for acquiring knowledge was the institution of pederasty, wherein the older male *erastēs* ('lover') was envisaged as educating and mentoring his younger male *erōmenos* ('beloved'). Both terms relate to the verb *erān* ('to desire'), and to Eros, the god (and the emotion) that presides over the symposium: Love in the sense of lust or desire. The *Symposium* describes two pederastic relationships, those of Callias and Autolycus, and of Critobulus and Cleinias (with Critobulus at 4.11–16 reporting the astonishing strength of his desire for his beloved). At the symposium Plato recounted, the guests had taken turns eulogizing Eros, whose connection with philosophy was also an interest of the Socratics more generally. Eros was generally understood by the ancient Greeks to be the representation of physical lust: his arrows implanted in their target an overpowering physical desire. As love in the sense of sexual desire, Eros was usually regarded as the polar opposite of *philia* (love in the sense of friendship); the two feelings, and their associated relationships, were considered incompatible.

It is near the end of Xenophon's work, in his long and climactic speech, that Socrates finally explicitly invokes the god and theme of Eros. Eros, he says, ought not to be ignored, since the guests are his devotees (VIII.1). But Socrates soon turns to demoting *erōs* in the sense of physical desire. He does so by invoking two contrasting Aphrodites, only one of which—the Popular—gives rise to physical desire. She should therefore be avoided. The other, Celestial Aphrodite, stimulates the far superior spiritual love: 'love of the soul, friendship, and noble [*kalon*] deeds' (VIII.10). (A speaker in Plato had invoked the same two Aphrodites, each possessing her own Eros, but mapped onto a different binary opposition: the one a shameful love aligned with heterosexuality, the other a more philosophical homoeroticism, 180c–181d.)

As the speech goes on, Xenophon has Socrates reimagine the institution of pederasty (in which the idea of *erōs* was ingrained in the very terms used) as potentially aligned with *philia* rather than *erōs*. This is a bold and surprising move, given the structural asymmetry of pederasty (wherein the active partner, the older *erastēs* ('lover'; the very term is active) was licensed to take enjoyment, while the younger *erōmenos* (passive 'beloved') was not), which one would expect to go against the grain of Xenophon's conception of reciprocal *philia*. Indeed, his Socrates characterizes physical homoerotic relationships as lacking in freedom (VIII.23), and explicitly counters (VIII.32–4) the idea expressed by Phaedrus in Plato's *Symposium* (178e–179b) of the band of male–male lovers as virtuous. Critobulus confirms the abject slavishness of this devotion in describing his desire for Cleinias (IV.14).

Socrates' desire to bring pederasty within the ambit of *philia* may explain why he outlaws any physical component in male–male homoerotic relationships. Intriguingly, there is no such outlawing of a physical dimension in the case of heterosexual relationships, which are presented as potentially conducive to reciprocal *philia* (despite the fact that sexual relationships between women and men were just as often envisaged as markedly unequal, with the often much younger wife viewed as taking a passive role). After decrying a physical sexual dimension in male homoerotic relationships, for the reason that it lacks reciprocal *philia* (VIII.19), Socrates remarks: 'For boys do not share in [*koinōnei*] the pleasure of sex with a man as women do, but remain sober while observing the intoxicated passion of someone else' (VIII.21). Socrates notes that Niceratus 'is in love with his wife, who reciprocates his feelings' (VIII.3) (lit. 'feels *erōs* for his wife, who feels *erōs* for him in return'), and the dialogue's closing scene arguably points to mutuality in the context of the clearly physical attraction felt between Ariadne and Dionysus (and, perhaps, the slave actors). Similarly, in *Estate Management*, the husband and wife are friends, yet their relationship is also physical (see especially X.10–12, where an exemplary Athenian husband coaches his young wife in how to be more sexually appealing).

So it is that Xenophon's Socrates endorses the manifold benefits of exclusively spiritual love in the case of Callias and Autolycus. Celestial love is aligned with friendship, and comes to look very much like it; and in the remainder of his speech Socrates eulogizes both these human associations or feelings. He remarks: 'We all know that without friendship there is no association worth mentioning' (VIII.13). Where physical love and appreciation for physical beauty may wane over time, spiritual love ('*philia* for the soul' (VIII.15)) brings a person right to old age still 'preserv(ing) their passion [*erōs*] for and enjoyment of friendship [*philia*]' (VIII.18). The appropriate role of *erōs*, then, is to be focused on *philia*: on friendship.

Socrates argues that one seeking friendship seeks to improve his beloved, and that the greatest good that comes to the person seeking to make his beloved a true friend is that he himself must cultivate virtue. Fine deeds are achieved by those willing to labour for the sake of praise; and Autolycus is such a one, who probably has ambitions to win broader praise, from friends and country and even foreigners (VIII.38). He will respect whomever he regards as most effective in helping him achieve this outcome—whoever understands how it is that civic bene-factors (Themistocles, Pericles, Solon) assist the city, and can there-fore assist him to do likewise. The speech culminates with Socrates' striking remark that 'just about all my life I have shared my city's pas-sion for (lit. "been a fellow-*erastēs* with the city of"") men who combine a noble nature with a keen desire for excellence' (VIII.41).

This alignment of pederasty with *philia* is part of a sustained strat-egy whereby Xenophon in this work stages a shift from *erōs* to *philia*, or the transformation of *erōs* into something closer to *philia*, so bring-ing closer together these normally incompatible relationships. Most remarkable is Socrates' invocation and transformation of the (erotic) metaphor of the pimp: for he seizes his listeners' attention by claim-ing to take most pride in this 'disreputable profession' (IV.56, cf. III.10), only to refigure the pimp's skill as the thoroughly beneficial capacity for bringing people together and making them attractive to one another (IV.59–60): for forging friendships between individuals and between individuals and the city. The metaphor is comical but nonetheless underscores the premium Socrates sets on relationships and furthers the idea that value may be found in unexpected places. In other ways too this symposium—which occurs under the sign of *erōs*—turns out to have *philia* as a guiding theme. Several of the evening's speeches revolve around *philia*. Hermogenes, for instance, takes most pride in his friendship with the gods, and his account of how he sustains that relationship over time (IV.49) captures Xenophon's conception of ideal *philia*. The theme of friendship and friendly relationships is sustained also in how the dialogue models and endorses a pleasant, respectful style of interaction, with a pre-mium set on agreement (see, e.g., IV.56–61). Socrates gently corrects Hermogenes for his disagreeable silence (VI.1–2). His interaction with the verbally abusive Syracusan is a model of moderate, humor-ous resistance. When others engage in more forceful reproach (VI.8), Socrates advises that they avoid being rude themselves (VI.9). Only Antisthenes employs the biting elenchus ('cross-examination', 'test-ing'; as at VI.5) characteristic of the Platonic Socrates. (Otherwise in this work, the term elenchus appears only in the passive: it is used of how a person's false reputation for virtue 'is examined' or 'exposed' by the test of real life (VIII.43). *Oec.* I.6–15 is an example of an elenchus in the sense of a series of questions and answers.)

After Socrates has finished his great speech, Callias takes up Socrates' striking metaphor, asking the philosopher to serve as a pimp between himself and the city, persuading him to enter politics and so earn her approval (VIII.42). Socrates replies:

Definitely . . . if people can see that your commitment to excellence is not pretended but genuine. False reputation is quickly exposed when put to the test, but true manly virtue, unless marred by some god, brings with it ever more glorious renown when supported by actions.

The comment that Callias will thus win 'more glorious' (*lamproterān*, lit. 'brighter') renown harks back to the dialogue's opening, where Callias was concerned to make his symposium 'more brilliant' (*lamproterān*). Socrates implies that, should Callias refocus his efforts towards the state, the private glamour he wins in hosting a splendid party will be eclipsed by an even brighter reputation in the eyes of the whole city. Socrates in this way encourages a turn towards the civic, refiguring spiritual *erōs* as something that can serve the public good. Xenophon thereby transforms the private venue of the symposium—site of elite connections and clubs that could be felt to work against the *polis* and its interests, and potentially even threaten the democracy—into a source of strength for the *polis*. Exemplary relationships are presented as an effective means to promote exemplary behaviour more generally, including in relation to the public sphere of the city.

It is an aspirational picture of what might have been—a Callias who rises beyond the plutocrat concerned to host a fancy party, instead to burnish the whole city more brightly—and finds a parallel in other Xenophontic works (so Hiero in the eponymous work has the potential to benefit not just himself but the whole community, and so make his city his friend and win great fame). The vision went unfulfilled but stands as a tribute to Socrates' commitment to the city—and therefore also as a compelling defence of the philosopher.

SHADOWS OF THE TRIAL OF SOCRATES

Alongside lighter elements—the party setting, the presence of a professional comic, the jokes—the work recalls and provides commentary on a historical event of utmost gravity: Socrates' trial and

execution. Like Xenophon's other Socratic works (most overtly the
Defence of Socrates (Apology) and *Memorabilia*), the *Symposium* is on
one level a defence of Socrates. It takes the remarkable step of bringing on stage an accuser figure and allowing Socrates to answer him.

The date of the work's action is the Great Panathenaea of 422 BCE
(as is easily established from the dates of plays in which the comic
poet Eupolis mocked the relationship of Callias and Autolycus). One
year earlier the comic poet Aristophanes had chosen Socrates to per-
sonify the negative, transgressive aspects of the contemporary sophists. Itinerant intellectuals of various stripes, several of the sophists
had an interest in rhetoric, and notoriously charged astronomical fees
to teach the art of persuasion to those desiring influence in the democracy. Aristophanes' decision was a clever one, dramatically, since
Socrates, unlike most sophists, resided in Athens. Headmaster of the
Thinkery, first glimpsed suspended on high in a basket, examining
meteorological phenomena, Socrates of *Clouds* is fixated on frivolous
topics such as measuring the distance a flea jumps, yet also responsible for contemporary social cataclysm. His school has disowned the
traditional gods in favour of new-fangled deities (Tongue, the Clouds)
and endorsed moral relativism, teaching students 'the worse argument'
at the expense of traditional values. The darkest of Aristophanic comedies, *Clouds* ends not on the usual note of jollity and restoration of
social cohesion, but with an act of violence as an angry student burns
down the school.

In Xenophon's *Symposium* the repulsive Syracusan slave master
pointedly recalls this portrait of Socrates (see also *Oec.* XI.3), which
Plato held responsible for cementing negative views that years later
played a role in securing Socrates' death sentence (*Apology* 18b–d,
19c). Envious of Socrates, since the guests are enjoying their own
company rather than his show, the slave master opens the following
conversation:

'Are you the one they call "The Thinker"?'

'Well, isn't that better', [Socrates] replied, 'than being known as "The
Thoughtless"?'

'Yes it would be, but only if you didn't have a reputation as a thinker about
higher things [things in mid-air/astronomical phenomena [*meteōrōn*]].'

'Do you know of anything higher [*meteōroteron*] than the gods?'

'Of course not; but that's not where people say your interests lie, but in
completely useless stuff.'

'Even if that were so, I might still be interested in the gods, since it's from up there that they send rain to help us and from up there that they provide our light. If you find this a dry answer, it's your fault for provoking me.'

'Well,' he said, 'let's not bother with that. Instead, tell me how many feet away from me a flea is. This is how people say you measure distances.' (VI.6–8)

Socrates flips on its head the Syracusan's accusation of impiety (one charge of the trial: cf. Xenophon, *Apology* 11–13), transforming it into proof of the reverse. (The traditional piety of Socrates and his disciples is highlighted elsewhere in the work, as in Hermogenes' speech (IV.47–8), a picture whose plausibility Socrates is made to endorse (IV.49).) The Syracusan's expression 'completely useless stuff' (*anōphelestatōn*, lit. 'most unhelpful') is the antonym of the epithet (*ōphelimos*, 'helpful') that Xenophon across his works attributes to Socrates in constructing his portrait of a man committed to benefiting the city. At this point other guests interject, not deigning to engage the Syracusan directly, but agreeing that he is obnoxious. Socrates checks them, to avoid the hypocrisy of themselves indulging in offensiveness, graciously thereby stifling the moment of unpleasantness.

Elsewhere the Syracusan slave master is the vehicle for raising the other main charge of the trial, that of corrupting the young. Invited to explain what he is most proud of, the Syracusan denies it is the slave-boy and confesses anxiety that 'people are plotting to ruin (or "corrupt", *diaphtheirai*)' the boy (IV.52) by sharing his bed. Socrates exposes his hypocrisy by drawing out the fact that the Syracusan himself sleeps with the boy every night. Indeed, the Syracusan comes to stand as a conspicuous foil to Socrates. The same charge against Socrates of corrupting the young is implicitly countered elsewhere in the work, where it is Socrates who redirects the proceedings away from the erotic appreciation of the beautiful young people and towards intellectual conversation (III.1–2), and argues at length for the moral superiority of celibacy—purely spiritual love—particularly in the context of homoerotic relationships (ch. 8).

The work also defends Socrates against the portrait of *Clouds* by joining Xenophon's other works, and Plato's, in constructing a strong opposition between Socrates and the Sophists: so the underscored contrast, in the opening scene, between Callias, who has paid exorbitant fees to learn from some of the most famous sophists of the day, and Socrates and his circle, whom he regards (so Socrates remarks) as 'amateurs in the matter of philosophy' (I.5). Hence too, perhaps, the emphasis on Socrates' poverty (he is clearly not taking large fees); and here as elsewhere Xenophon presents a Socrates whose overriding interest is in questions of ethics and morality. At *Memorabilia* 1.1.11–16 he records Socrates' criticism of those who speculated on celestial phenomena. Did they regard their knowledge of human affairs (*ta anthrōpina*) as so complete that they needed to find other topics on which to ruminate?

The significance of Socrates' trial and its outcome continues to be debated today (was it mostly a matter of religion? Of politics and recent history? Of freedom of speech?), but there is no question that the turbulent events of the late fifth century BCE are crucial to its understanding. For why—when any citizen at Athens could file an indictment—did no one file a complaint against Socrates until he was 70 years old? In the later stages of the Peloponnesian War an oligarchic coup (411 BCE) briefly put The Four Hundred into power, then, upon Sparta's decisive defeat of Athens (in 404 BCE), the assembly voted to end the democracy and submit to the rule of The Thirty, a junta that governed Athens in the interests of Sparta. Cruel and greedy in executing citizens and depriving people of property and basic rights, The Thirty soon earned the designation Thirty Tyrants. The democratic opposition eventually defeated their forces in battle, democracy was restored, and amnesty from prosecution for illegal actions committed previously was given to all but The Thirty and some others. But it was regarded as suspicious to have stayed in the city, as had Socrates, and not to have joined the resistance (though Plato reports Socrates' refusal to obey one of The Thirty's orders (*Apology* 32c–d), and Xenophon his open criticism of The Thirty (*Memorabilia* 1.2.32)). Particularly disquieting was Socrates' earlier association with some of the key players as teacher and mentor, notably Critias—The Thirty's murderous leader—and Alcibiades, who had caused real damage to Athens by switching sides in the war. Writing some decades later, Xenophon and Plato both make the case that, while these individuals associated with Socrates, he kept them on the straight and narrow (see, e.g., Xenophon, *Memorabilia* 1.2.12–39). But, with Athens defeated and occupied by a Spartan army, and the democracy suspended and replaced by a pro-Spartan oligarchy, with Critias at its centre, one can imagine how Socrates began to seem more subversive.

Several of those depicted in Xenophon's *Symposium* were connected to the oligarchic ringleaders or in other ways involved in those late-fifth-century events. Charmides, cousin of Critias and one of the ten commissioners of The Thirty who governed Peiraeus (*Hellenica* 2.4.19), would be killed fighting on their side. In the *Symposium* he refers to himself as 'a kind of tyrant' now that he has lost his wealth (IV.32). His impoverishment was the upshot of his being implicated, along with Alcibiades and Critias, in an earlier religious scandal (in 415 BCE). Autolycus and Niceratus were eliminated by the Thirty Tyrants or their Spartan sponsors. A few years later, Autolycus' father Lycon would be one of Socrates' accusers. Hermogenes, Antisthenes, and Critobulus (the same man who received Socrates' advice in *Estate Management*), disciples of Socrates, would be present when he drank the hemlock.

For readers aware of all these connections—and at least some contemporary readers must have been—these future events darken the shadow cast over what might seem initially a thoroughly light-hearted work.

FACT OR FICTION?

In some ways, then, Xenophon's dialogue has its basis in history. But how far does the dialogue describe events that actually occurred on an evening in 422 BCE? As noted earlier, Socratic dialogues are likely to be fictional in essence, and Xenophon cannot have been present at this symposium, as the narrator claims (*Symposium* I.1).

Like Jesus or Muhammad, Socrates wrote nothing down, but his followers were inspired to take up the pen. The contrasting images of Socrates in Xenophon and Plato (not to mention Aristophanes' comic take in *Clouds*) have precipitated decades of debate on the 'Socratic problem', the question of what the historical Socrates was really like. The likely fictional nature of the *logoi Sōkratikoi* makes this a challenging and possibly fruitless endeavour. More productive may be to analyse each individual construction of Socrates, the themes it explores, and how and to what extent it may reflect on contemporary events. At the same time, each disciple of Socrates who turned author probably captured a different facet of the real Socrates' personality, teachings, and approach. Xenophon's Socratic works are a worthy contribution.

TRANSLATOR'S NOTE

XENOPHON was renowned in antiquity for the simplicity, grace, and purity of his Attic style. He therefore presents his translator with few problems.

As one would expect, these two works are mostly in a conversational register, interspersed with passages of exposition. Some of the latter may show signs of Xenophon's mild tendency towards repetition; but one can never be sure he is not allowing himself a touch of characterization. For example, when Ischomachus is explaining to his young wife the principle of 'everything in its place' in their house, he takes twelve sections (*Oec.* 8.18–23) to pile on the illustrations. She might well have taken the point long before he exclaims bathetically on the beauty in their storeroom of a neatly arranged row of shoes or cooking pots. Ischomachus is nothing if not earnest.

Symposium is among other things a brilliant exercise in lively character study; the participants' strengths and weaknesses are neatly sketched, often with gentle humour—except for the Syracusan showman, who is of course not an Athenian gentleman, and perhaps the freeloading Philip. At IV.59 we have what looks like a rare Greek joke, when some guests chorus an inane answer to Socrates' question: either an ironic comment on the power of his interrogation, or perhaps a sly metatextual dig at a cliché of philosophical dialogue.

Xenophon gives both these works a formal unity by building discussion round a recurrent key concept: in *Estate Management* it is *epimeleia*, and in *Symposium kalokagathia*.

The former's semantic range includes 'care, application, diligence, practice, taking pains'. I have found it impossible to confine myself to a single word or derivative to render this unifying idea into English, but Emily Baragwanath's excellent Introduction and Notes always draw the reader's attention to points where Xenophon's intention needs to be recognized.

As to the latter, a wholly ancient Greek notion without parallel in English, I have used the quaint word 'gentlemanliness', mainly to remind the reader that we are here faced with a view of ideal breeding and behaviour that requires some mental dislocation to understand it. Once again, the Introduction and Notes enable the student to leap the gap of 2,500 years. The Greek text I have used is E.C. Marchant's second Oxford edition (1921), with some small adjustements.

I am very grateful to Emily [Baragwanath] for her scholarship and practical suggestions, which both corrected mistakes and improved the clarity of my version. Any surviving inaccuracies and infelicities are entirely my responsibility.

SELECT BIBLIOGRAPHY

Xenophon's Life

Anderson, J. K., *Xenophon* (New York, Scribner, 1974) (on Xenophon's life).

Flower, Michael A., *Xenophon's* Anabasis, *or, the* Expedition of Cyrus (New York: Oxford University Press, 2012) (excellent introduction to Xenophon and his autobiographical *Anabasis*).

Lee, John W. I., 'Xenophon and his Times', in Michael A. Flower (ed.), *The Cambridge Companion to Xenophon* (Cambridge: Cambridge University Press, 2017), 15–36.

Tuplin, Christopher, 'Xenophon and Athens', in Michael A. Flower (ed.), *The Cambridge Companion to Xenophon* (Cambridge: Cambridge University Press, 2017), 338–59.

Literary Studies

Azoulay, Vincent, *Xenophon and the Graces of Power: A Greek Guide to Political Manipulation* (Swansea: The Classical Press of Wales, 2018); trans. from French original (2004) (important study of the notion *charis* (gratitude, grace, reciprocity) in Xenophon's oeuvre).

Berkel, Tazuko Angela van, *The Economics of Friendship* (Leiden: Brill, 2020) (ch. 5 on friendship according to Xenophon's Socrates).

Buxton, Richard Fernando, 'Xenophon on Leadership: Commanders as Friends', in Michael A. Flower (ed.), *The Cambridge Companion to Xenophon* (Cambridge: Cambridge University Press, 2017), 323–37.

Danzig, Gabriel, Johnson, David M., and Morrison, Donald R. (eds), *Plato and Xenophon* (Leiden and Boston: Brill, 2018) (a useful collection of comparative essays; the introductory essay by Danzig considers the nature of the interactions between the works of Xenophon and Plato).

Dorion, Louis-André, 'The Straussian Exegesis of Xenophon', in Vivienne J. Gray (ed.), *Xenophon* (Oxford Readings in Classical Studies; Oxford and New York: Oxford University Press, 2010), 283–323.

Flower, Michael A. (ed.), *The Cambridge Companion to Xenophon* (Cambridge: Cambridge University Press, 2017 (a useful collection of essays).

Gray, Vivienne J. (ed.) *Xenophon* (Oxford Readings in Classical Studies; Oxford and New York: Oxford University Press, 2010) (a useful collection of essays).

Gray, Vivienne J., *Xenophon's Mirror of Princes: Reading the Reflections* (Oxford and New York: Oxford University Press, 2011) (treatment of the literary techniques Xenophon uses to represent leadership throughout his works; with critique of Straussian readings).

Johnson, David M., 'Strauss on Xenophon', in Christopher Tuplin and Fiona Hobden (eds), *Xenophon: Ethical Principles and Historical Enquiry* (Leiden and Boston: Brill, 2012), 123–59.

Johnson, David M., *Xenophon's Socratic Works* (Routledge Monographs in Classical Studies; Abingdon and New York: Routledge, 2021) (includes discussion of Xenophon's Socrates' moral psychology (ch. 4), *Symposium* (ch. 5), and *Estate Management* (ch. 6)).

Pangle, Thomas L., *Socrates Founding Political Philosophy in Xenophon's Economist, Symposium, and* Apology (Chicago and London: University of Chicago Press, 2020) (a Straussian reading, including of *Estate Management* (pp. 7–119) and *Symposium* (pp. 120–44)).

Pelling, Christopher, 'Xenophon's Authorial Voice', in Michael A. Flower (ed.), *The Cambridge Companion to Xenophon* (Cambridge: Cambridge University Press, 2017), 241–62.

Socrates

Danzig, Gabriel, 'Introduction to the Comparative Study of Plato and Xenophon', in Gabriel Danzig, David M. Johnson, and Donald R. Morrison (eds), *Plato and Xenophon* (Leiden and Boston: Brill, 2018), 1–30 (at pp. 8–18 helpfully reviews the 'Socratic Question': whether and how far either Xenophon or Plato provides a faithful reflection of the historical Socrates).

Dorion, Louis-André, 'Xenophon's Socrates', in Sara Ahbel-Rappe and Rachana Kamtekar (eds), *A Companion to Socrates* (Malden and Oxford: Blackwell Publishing, 2006), 93–109.

Gray, Vivienne J., 'Xenophon's Socrates on Democracy', *Polis*, 28/1 (2011), 1–32.

Johnson, David M., 'Xenophon's Intertextual Socrates', in Gabriel Danzig, David M. Johnson, and Donald R. Morrison (eds), *Plato and Xenophon* (Leiden and Boston: Brill, 2018), 71–98.

Morrison, Donald R., 'Xenophon's Socrates as Teacher', in P. A. Vander Waerdt (ed.), *The Socratic Movement* (Ithaca, NY: Cornell University Press, 1994), 181–208; republished in Vivienne J. Gray (ed.), *Xenophon* (Oxford Readings in Classical Studies; Oxford and New York: Oxford University Press, 2010), 195–227.

Morrison, Donald R., 'On Professor Vlastos' Xenophon', *Ancient Philosophy*, 7 (1987): 9–22 (defending Xenophon and his portrait of Socrates against an influential critic's charge of dullness and conventionality).

Morrison, Donald R. (ed.), *The Cambridge Companion to Socrates* (Cambridge: Cambridge University Press, 2011) (a useful collection of essays).

Nails, Debra, *The People of Plato: A Prosopography of Plato and Other Socratics* (Indianapolis: Hackett Publishing, 2002) (includes helpful information about the historical individuals who appear in the works included in this volume).

Estate Management

Baragwanath, Emily, 'The Wonder of Freedom: Xenophon on Slavery', in Christopher Tuplin and Fiona Hobden (eds), *Xenophon: Ethical Principle and Historical Enquiry* (Leiden and Boston: Brill, 2012), 631–63 (pp. 645–9 on *Estate Management*).

Carlsen, J., 'Estate Managers in Ancient Greek Agriculture', in Jens Erik Skydsgaard and Karen Ascani (eds), *Ancient History Matters: Studies*

Presented to Jens Erik Skydsgaard on his Seventieth Birthday (Analecta Romana Instituti Danici, Supplementum, 30; Rome: L'Erma di Bretschneider, 2002), 117–26.

Danzig, Gabriel, 'Why Socrates was not a Farmer: Xenophon's *Oeconomicus* as a Philosophical Dialogue', *Greece & Rome*, 50 (2003), 57–76.

Foucault, Michel, *The History of Sexuality, vol. 2: The Use of Pleasure*, trans. R. Hurley (New York: Vintage Books, 1985) (pp. 152–65 on *Estate Management*)

Gini, Anthony, 'The Manly Intellect of his Wife: Xenophon *Oeconomicus* Ch. 7', *Classical World*, 86/6 (1993), 483–6.

Glazebrook, Allison, 'Cosmetics and *Sōphrosunē*: Ischomachos' Wife in Xenophon's *Oikonomikos*', *Classical World*, 102/3 (2009), 233–48.

Goldhill, Simon, *Foucault's Virginity: Ancient Erotic Fiction and the History of Sexuality* (Cambridge: Cambridge University Press, 1995) (pp. 139–41 on *Estate Management*).

Hobden, Fiona, 'Xenophon's *Oeconomicus*', in Michal A. Flower (ed.), *The Cambridge Companion to Xenophon* (Cambridge: Cambridge University Press, 2017), 152–73 (helpful Appendix, pp. 168–73, on Ischomachus' wife Chrysilla and her bearing on the work's interpretation).

Johnstone, Steven, 'Virtuous Toil, Vicious Work: Xenophon on Aristocratic Style', *Classical Philology*, 89 (1994), 219–40 (pp. 229–35 on *Estate Management*).

Kronenberg, Leah, *Allegories of Farming from Greece and Rome: Philosophical Satire in Xenophon, Varro and Virgil* (Cambridge and New York: Cambridge University Press, 2009) (pp. 37–72 on *Estate Management*).

Lacey, Walter K., *The Family in Classical Greece* (London: Thames & Hudson, 1968).

Murnaghan, Sheila, 'How a Woman Can Be More Like a Man: The Dialogue between Ischomachus and his Wife in Xenophon's *Oeconomicus*', *Helios*, 15 (1988), 9–22.

North, Helen, 'The Mare, the Vixen, and the Bee: Sophrosyne as the Virtue of Women in Antiquity', *ICS* 2 (1977), 35–48 (Xenophon's originality in defining *sōphrosunē* with reference to household management (p. 46)).

Pelling, Christopher, *Literary Texts and the Greek Historian* (London and New York: Routledge, 2000) (discussion of *Estate Management* and its 'rhetoric of masculine control' (p. 241) at pp. 236–45).

Pomeroy, Sarah B., 'Slavery in the Greek Domestic Economy in the Light of Xenophon's *Oeconomicus*', *Index*, 17 (1989), 11–18, republished in Vivienne J. Gray (ed.), *Xenophon* (Oxford Readings in Classical Studies; Oxford and New York: Oxford University Press, 2010), 31–40.

Pomeroy, Sarah B., *Xenophon, Oeconomicus: A Social and Historical Commentary* (Oxford and New York: Oxford University Press, 1994).

Scaife, Ross, 'Ritual and Persuasion in the House of Ischomachus', *Classical Journal*, 90/3 (1995), 225–32.

Stevens, J., 'Friendship and Profit in Xenophon's *Oeconomicus*', in P. A. Vander Waerdt (ed.), *The Socratic Movement* (Ithaca, NY: Cornell University Press, 1994), 209–37.

Strauss, Leo, *Xenophon's Socratic Discourse: An Interpretation of the* Oeconomicus (Ithaca, NY: Cornell University Press, 1970) (a highly controversial but influential reading).

Too, Yun Lee, 'The Economies of Pedagogy: Xenophon's Wifely Didactics', *Proceedings of the Cambridge Philological Association*, 47 (2001), 65–80.

Symposium

Bowen, Anthony (ed.), *Xenophon* Symposium (Warminster: Aris & Phillips, 1998).

Danzig, Gabriel, 'Intra-Socratic Polemics: The *Symposia* of Plato and Xenophon', *Greek, Roman, and Byzantine Studies*, 45 (2005), 331–57.

Danzig, Gabriel, 'Xenophon's *Symposium*', in Michal A. Flower (ed.), *The Cambridge Companion to Xenophon* (Cambridge: Cambridge University Press, 2017), 132–51.

Dover, Kenneth J., *Greek Homosexuality* (London: Duckworth, 1978).

Dover, Kenneth J., *Plato:* Symposium (Cambridge and New York: Cambridge University Press, 1980).

Halliwell, Stephen, *Greek Laughter: A Study of Cultural Psychology from Homer to Early Christianity* (Cambridge and New York: Cambridge University Press, 2008) (pp. 139–54 on Xenophon's *Symposium*).

Higgins, William Edward, *Xenophon the Athenian: The Problem of the Individual and the Society of the Polis* (Albany, NY: State University of New York Press, 1977) (pp. 15–20 on Xenophon's *Symposium*).

Hindley, Clifford, 'Xenophon on Male Love', *Classical Quarterly*, 49 (1999), 74–99, republished in Vivienne J. Gray (ed.), *Xenophon* (Oxford Readings in Classical Studies; Oxford and New York: Oxford University Press, 2010), 72–110.

Hobden, Fiona, *The Symposion in Ancient Greek Society and Thought* (Cambridge: Cambridge University Press, 2013) (ch. 5 on Plato's and Xenophon's *Symposium*).

Hunter, Richard, *Plato's* Symposium (Oxford and New York: Oxford University Press, 2004) (helpful on Plato's *Symposium*, the institution of the symposium, on *erōs*, and further bibliography).

Huss, Bernhard, 'The Dancing Sokrates and the Laughing Xenophon, or the Other Symposium', *American Journal of Philology*, 120/3 (1999), 381–409; republished in Vivienne J. Gray (ed.), *Xenophon* (Oxford Readings in Classical Studies; Oxford and New York: Oxford University Press, 2010), 257–82.

Pentassuglio, Francesca, 'Socrates *Erotikos*: Mutuality, Role Reversal, and Erotic *Paideia* in Xenophon's and Plato's *Symposia*', in Gabriel Danzig, David M. Johnson, and Donald R. Morrison (eds), *Plato and Xenophon* (Leiden and Boston: Brill, 2018), 364–90.

Thesleff, Holger, 'The Interrelation and Date of the *Symposia* of Plato and Xenophon', *Bulletin of the Institute of Classical Studies*, 25 (1978), 157–70.

Thomsen, Ole, 'Socrates and Love', *Classica et Mediaevalia*, 52 (2001), 117–78.

Wohl, Victoria, 'Dirty Dancing', in Penelope Murray and Peter Wilson (eds), *Music and the Muses: The Culture of 'mousikē' in the Classical Athenian City* (Oxford and New York: Oxford University Press, 2004), 337–63.

ESTATE MANAGEMENT

I

I ONCE also heard him* talking about estate management.* This is how the conversation went:

Tell me, Critobulus,* he said, is estate management the name of a branch of knowledge,* like medicine or smithing or carpentry?

I think so, said Critobulus.

Then are we able to say what its function is, just as we can describe 2 the function of these other occupations?

Well, he said, I suppose the function of a good estate manager is to manage his estate well.

So if someone were to be entrusted with another man's estate, would 3 he not be able to manage it as well as his own, if he wanted to? After all, someone who knows about carpentry could work for another person just as well as for himself; and the same would apply to estate management.

Yes, I think so, Socrates.*

In that case it's possible for a man who has this skill, even if he has 4 no property of his own, to earn money by managing someone else's estate, just as he might do by building him a house?

Of course he could, said Critobulus, and a lot of money too, if, after taking on the estate and paying the necessary bills, he created a surplus and so increased its value.

What do we understand by the word 'estate'? Is it simply a house, 5 or does it include everything a person possesses outside his house? Is that all part of the estate?

My view, said Critobulus, is that, even if they do not lie in the same city as himself, all of a man's possessions count as part of his estate.

And do some people possess enemies?   6

They certainly do—many in some cases.

Are we then to say that his enemies count as his possessions?

It would surely be absurd, said Critobulus, if someone was paid money for increasing the number of a person's enemies!

Except, said Socrates, that we thought a man's estate was the same 7 as his property.

Of course, but only if it is a good kind of property. There is absolutely no way I would use the word property for any bad thing he possesses.

Perhaps you mean by property what is useful* to its possessor.

I do. I think things that are harmful produce loss rather than wealth.*

8   I suppose, then, that if someone buys a horse but doesn't know how to handle it,* and keeps falling off and injuring himself, that horse is not to be counted as wealth for him?

Not if it's true that wealth is a good.

So not even land counts as wealth for someone if he works it in such a way as to produce a loss?

True—not even land is wealth if, instead of sustaining you, it causes you to starve.

9   Does the same principle also apply to sheep? If a man incurs loss by not knowing how to treat them,* they would not count as wealth for him?

They wouldn't, in my opinion.

It follows, then, that you consider beneficial things* to be wealth, and harmful things to be the opposite?

Yes.

10   So it is true that the same things represent wealth for someone who knows how to use them in each case, but the opposite of wealth for someone who doesn't. Take flutes,* for example: for someone
11   who can play the instrument tolerably well owning it represents wealth, while for someone who can't it is no better than a useless stone—unless he sells it. From which it follows that for those who can't play it selling a flute represents wealth, but not if they keep it instead of selling it.

Yes, Socrates. There is a consistency in the way our discussion is moving, since we did in fact agree that things that benefit us* count as wealth. A flute that is not offered for sale is not wealth, because it is useless, but becomes wealth when it is sold.

Socrates said in answer:

12   Yes, but only if the owner knows how to sell it. But again, if he were to sell it in exchange for something he doesn't know how to use, even when it's sold it wouldn't count as wealth, according to your argument.

You seem to be saying, Socrates, that not even money counts as wealth unless you know how to use it.

And you seem to agree with me that only what can benefit us can be 13 considered as wealth. For example, suppose someone used his money to buy a concubine,* which resulted in him being worse off in body, soul and estate, how could his money be beneficial to him?

It can't—unless we also maintain that the plant called henbane, which drives people who eat it out of their mind, is wealth.

Money, then, Critobulus, if you don't know how to use it, should 14 be banished so far away from you that it actually ceases to be wealth. But what about friends?* If someone knows how to use them in such a way that they benefit him, what shall we say they are?

That they are wealth, of course, and much more so than cattle, if it's true that they are more beneficial than cattle.

Enemies, too, according to your argument, must be counted as 15 wealth, if you know how to use them.

Well, *I* think so.

It is then the mark of a good estate manager that he knows how to treat enemies so as to derive benefit from them.

Most certainly.

And you must of course be aware, Critobulus, that a large number of private citizens' estates, as well as those of tyrants,* have been enlarged by war.

Yes, I think that must be true, said Critobulus. But there is also the 16 fact that we sometimes see people who have the knowledge and resources to enable them (if they work at it) to enlarge their households, and yet we find that they are unwilling to do so, and because of this we see that their knowledge is no use to them. It must follow that neither their knowledge nor their property is actually wealth.

Are you trying, said Socrates, to have a discussion with me about 17 slaves?*

No, certainly not; I'm talking about people regarded as being of the highest birth. What I observe is that, though some of them are skilled in the arts of war and others in those of peacetime, they are unwilling to cultivate these, simply because—as it seems to me—they have no masters.

But how can it be that they have no masters, said Socrates, when, 18 in spite of praying for prosperity and being willing to do what will benefit them, they are prevented from achieving their aims by those who rule them?

Oh come, said Critobulus. Who are these invisible masters?

19   They are by no means invisible, said Socrates, but very clear to see.
They are also extremely vicious, as you are doubtless aware, at least if
20 you regard laziness, moral infirmity, and negligence as vices. And
there are also some deceitful mistresses that pretend to be pleasures,
such as gambling and keeping unprofitable company; with the passage of time it becomes abundantly clear even to those deceived by
them that they are really pains thinly disguised as pleasures, which by
exercising domination over them prevent them from undertaking any
profitable activity.*

21   Yes, Socrates, but there are other people who are not hindered
from working hard by these masters and have a strong drive towards
industriousness and towards ways of making money; yet despite this
they impoverish their estates and become entangled in difficulties.

22   Yes, because they too are slaves, and their masters are particularly
cruel. Some are in thrall to gluttony, some to lechery, some to drunkenness, some to senseless and expensive ambition. The rule of these
vices is so harsh that, when they gain control of a person, so long as
they can see he is healthy and capable of work, they force him to hand
over the fruits of his labour in order to feed their own desires; but,
when they observe that he is incapable of work through advanced
years, they abandon him to a miserable old age and try to make slaves
23 of others. No, Critobulus, we must fight for our freedom against these
as hard as against those who attempt to enslave us by force of arms. In
fact, enemies may well be gentlemen* too, who in the process of
enslaving their opponents teach them a lesson in moderation* and
force them to improve themselves and to live more temperate lives in
the future. Mistresses of the kind I describe, however, do constant
outrage to men's bodies and souls,* and to their estates, for as long as
they have control over them.

II

CRITOBULUS' next contribution was more or less on these lines.

Well, I think you have given me a more than adequate account of
weaknesses of these kinds, and when I examine myself I reckon I have
them pretty well under control;* so that if you will advise me what
I should now do to increase my estate I don't think I shall be prevented by these mistresses, as you call them. So don't hold back, and

give me whatever good advice you have—or perhaps in your judgement, Socrates, we are already wealthy enough, and in your view
don't need any more money?

If you are talking about me as well, I certainly don't think *I* need 2
any more money, as I am rich enough. You, however, Critobulus, seem
to me to be exceedingly poor; indeed, there are times when I feel very
sorry for you.

Critobulus laughed at this, and said:

Good heavens, Socrates, how much do you think your property 3
would fetch in a sale, and how much would mine?

Well, if I found a good buyer, I reckon everything I own, including
my house, would fetch at least five minas.* As to yours, I'm sure it
would sell for more than a hundred times that much.

And yet, knowing this, you don't consider you are in need of more 4
money, whereas you pity me for my poverty?

Yes, because my property is sufficient to answer my needs,* whereas
I don't think that even if your fortune increased to three times its
present size you would have enough to support the lifestyle you have
adopted, or your reputation.

What do you mean? said Critobulus. 5

I mean, explained Socrates, that in the first place you feel compelled to make a lot of large sacrifices; if you didn't, I imagine you
would get on the wrong side of both gods and men. Second, you are
obliged to entertain many guests from abroad,* and lavishly at that.
And, third, you also have to invite fellow citizens to dinner and act as
their benefactor, or else lose their support. What is more, I notice that 6
the city makes many financial demands on you:* you have to keep
horses, to pay for dramatic choruses and athletic competitions, and
hold civic chairmanships. And if war breaks out, I know that its officials will make you responsible for maintaining a trireme and will levy
more taxes of this kind than you can afford. If ever they think your
performance of these duties is less than adequate, I know that the
Athenians will punish you exactly as if they had caught you stealing 7
from them. On top of all this, I observe that you think of yourself as
a wealthy man and so show little interest in actually making money;
and yet you avidly carry on liaisons with boys as if you had plenty.
That is why I pity you, for I fear you will suffer some misfortune for
which there is no cure, and fall into hopeless penury. In my case, how- 8
ever, if I should want even a little more than I possess, you know as

well as I do that there are people who would help me, and whose tiny
contributions would swamp my life in riches—whereas your friends,
who are far more capable of supporting their style of life than you are
yours, nevertheless look to *you* to help *them* out.

9   Critobulus said: I can't argue with you on that point, Socrates. But
it's time for you to take on the role of my patron, so that I don't really
become an object of pity.

In answer Socrates said:

Don't you find it extraordinary, Critobulus, that a few moments
ago, when I said that I was wealthy, you laughed at me as if I didn't
know what the word meant. You kept on until you proved me wrong,*
and forced me to admit that I didn't own even one-hundredth of your
possessions—and now you're telling me to act as your patron and do
what I can to prevent* you actually becoming a pauper.*

10   True, Socrates; and I can see that you understand one way to
increase wealth, that is, how to create a surplus. I imagine that anyone
who can make a surplus from small beginnings can very easily make
a very large one from large resources.

11   Then don't you remember saying, when we were talking just now,
and when you wouldn't let me get a word in edgeways, that if a person
cannot manage horses they do not count as wealth for him, nor do
land or sheep or money or anything else, if he doesn't know how to
handle them? It is these sources that produce income, so how
do you suppose I could handle them when I have never owned any
of them?

12   But we decided that even if a man owns no wealth there is nevertheless a branch of knowledge called estate management. So is there
anything to stop you too acquiring this knowledge?

The very same reason, don't you see, said Socrates, that prevents
a man knowing how to play the flute if he's never owned one himself,
or if no one has ever lent him one to learn on. That is exactly my

13 position with estate management. I've never had enough money to
have an instrument to learn on, nor has anyone ever given me the
chance to handle one of his, except that just now you were prepared
to offer me yours. Beginners in lyre playing can, I imagine, actually
damage their instruments, and so if I was to try and learn how to
manage an estate by practising on yours I could very well ruin it
irrevocably.

14   Critobulus replied:

It's obvious, Socrates, that you're doing everything you can to avoid helping me bear my burdensome duties more easily.

No, no, not at all. I'm more than willing to pass on to you all I know. Supposing you had run out of fire and came to my house, and I didn't have any but took you to a place where you could get it, I don't think you would hold that against me; or if you were looking for water and I didn't have any myself but took you somewhere else for it, I don't think you would blame me for that either; or, again, if you wanted to learn music with me, and I pointed you towards people who were far more skilled in music than me, and who would be grateful to you for taking lessons with them; how could you possibly blame me for that?

I couldn't, Socrates, in all fairness.*

In that case I shall direct you to those who are far more skilful than I am in all those subjects that you are now anxious to learn from me. I must admit that I have gone to some trouble to identify the most knowledgeable in the city in each of these disciplines. I have in the past been amazed to discover that the same activity can make people either extremely poor or extremely rich, and so I decided that it was worth investigating why this should be so. When I looked into it I found that there is a natural explanation for this: I saw that those who follow their interests without proper thought suffer loss, while those who concentrate on applying themselves achieve their aims more quickly, easily, and profitably. So I reckon that if you too chose to learn from these people you could—unless some god opposes you—turn into a successful businessman.

III

IN answer Critobulus said:

You may be sure, Socrates, that I'll never let you go until you've proved what you have promised me in front of all these friends here.

Very well, Critobulus. To begin with, what if I can prove to you that some people spend a great deal of money on building houses that are useless while others build houses at much less expense that have every convenience? Will you agree that I am thereby illustrating for you one of the principles of estate management?

Certainly.

And if I go on to show you something that follows from this:

there are people who own a lot of furniture and objects of all kinds, but
cannot lay their hands on it when they need it, and don't even know if it
is safely stored, which is a constant source of annoyance both to themselves and their slaves.* And yet there are others who possess no more,
but even less, and yet have whatever they need immediately ready for use.

3   The reason for this, Socrates, must be that the former throw
everything down anywhere, while the latter keep each item stored in
its place.

Absolutely—and not of course where it just happens to be, but put
away in its designated location.

I assume you are saying that this too is a part of estate management?

4   And what if I go on to give you the example of slaves*—that in
some households nearly all of them are held in chains and yet keep
running away, whereas in others they have some freedom and are willing to work and remain at their stations? Wouldn't you think that this
too is an aspect of estate management that is worth looking into?*

Yes, very much so, said Critobulus.

5   Then take farming: do some men claim they are reduced to poverty
by farming, while others who work the same kind of land do very well
from their business and have an abundance of all they need?

Undeniably. Perhaps some spend money not only on necessities
but also on what brings harm to both master and estate.

6   Yes, there may be people like that; but I wasn't talking about them,
but about those who claim to be farmers but can't even raise the
money to meet their necessary expenditure.

What would be the reason for that, Socrates?

I'll take you to visit them too, and when you see them you will I'm
sure understand.

I'm sure I shall—if I'm able to, that is.

7   Then you must watch and examine yourself to see if you do understand. When there are comedies being performed I've known you to
get up very early and walk a very long way to see one, and you do your
best to persuade me to go to the theatre with you; but you have never
yet invited me to watch a performance like the one I've mentioned.*

You must think I cut a ridiculous figure, Socrates.

8   But not as ridiculous as you think, I assure you! I could show you
that some men have ended up in poverty as a result of keeping horses,
while others grow rich by doing so and also pride themselves on the
profit they make.

Well, I too see them, and I'm aware of both sorts; but it doesn't mean I'm any more likely to join the profit-makers.

It's because you watch them in the same way as you watch actors in 9 tragedy and comedy—not, I think, with a view to becoming a playwright but to derive pleasure from seeing and hearing. And perhaps this is right, because you have no wish to become a writer. But since you are actually forced to deal with horses, don't you think it foolish of you not to find out how to acquire more than a layman's knowledge of this business, especially when the very same horses are both good to use and profitable to sell?

So you think I should take up breaking in colts, Socrates? 10

Of course not, any more than you should buy farmers and train them up from childhood. But there are, I think, specific ages at which both horses and men suddenly become useful* and then continue to improve. I could also demonstrate to you how the way that some men treat their wives turns them into co-workers and partners in increasing their estate, while others' behaviour results in complete disaster.*

Should one blame the husband or the wife for that, Socrates? 11

If a sheep is sick, we usually blame the shepherd, and if a horse turns vicious, we usually say it's the rider's fault. In the case of a wife, however, if she has been instructed by her husband in good behaviour but then conducts herself badly, she might reasonably* be blamed for it; but if he doesn't teach her how to do things properly and then finds her ignorant, shouldn't he be held responsible? But anyway, 12 Critobulus, we're all friends here, and so you must tell us the truth; is there anyone to whom you entrust more matters of importance than to your wife?

No one.

Is there anyone with whom you talk* less than with your wife?

No one—or not many, at any rate.

And you married her when she was still very young,* and had seen 13 or heard very little of the world?

I certainly did.

Then it would be much more surprising if she knew what to say or do than if she made mistakes.

But what about those husbands, Socrates, who you say have good 14 wives? Did they train* them themselves?

There's nothing like looking at examples. I shall introduce Aspasia* to you, who is far more knowledgeable than I am in this matter and

15 will explain* it all to you. In my view, a wife who is a good partner in
the household has as much influence on its prosperity as her husband.*
As a general rule, wealth comes into a house as a result of the husband's
activities, but its expenditure is controlled mainly by his wife's stew-
ardship. When both do their jobs well, the estate prospers, but if they
are incompetent, its wealth diminishes. If you think you need further
16 proof of this in the case of other branches of knowledge, I believe
I can point you towards people whose achievements in any one of
them are worthy of record.*

IV

WHY do you need to mention them all, Socrates? It isn't easy to find
workmen who are competent in every skill, nor to master them all
oneself. Could you please indicate to me those branches of knowledge
that are considered the noblest,* and which it would be particularly
suitable for me to cultivate,* and also point out people who are
engaged in them, and give me as much help as you can yourself in
mastering them?
2   Well, Critobulus, that makes good sense. As we know, the so-called
banausic* occupations are looked down on, and perhaps justifiably
have a poor reputation in cities. They ruin the bodies of both labourers and foremen, forcing them to sit still and avoid sunlight, and in
some cases to spend the whole day near a fire. As their bodies become
effeminate, so too their souls lose most of their strength. Furthermore,
3 these so-called banausic occupations allow no spare time to attend to
the interests of their friends or their city; and so men of this kind are
considered useless at looking after their friends or defending their
country.* In fact, in some cities, especially those with a good reputation in warfare,* it is not even permitted to any citizen to work at
banausic occupations.
4   Which ones then, Socrates, would you recommend us to take up?
       We should surely not be ashamed to imitate the King of the
Persians?* They say that he considers farming and warfare to be
among the most glorious and essential professions there are, and
consequently devotes vigorous attention* to both.
5   Do you really believe that the Persian King counts farming among
his activities?

If we look at it in the following way, we may perhaps discover if he does. We agree that he does apply himself energetically to military matters, because he has laid down instructions to every governor of peoples who pay him tribute as to the number of horsemen, archers, slingers, and light-armed soldiers he must equip, sufficient to control those under his rule and also to defend his territory in case of an enemy invasion. Apart from these, the King maintains garrisons in his citadels. The upkeep of these troops is entrusted to the com- 6 mander whose duty this is, but every year the King holds a review of the mercenaries and others ordered to carry arms. He assembles everyone except those in citadels at the place called the muster, per- sonally inspecting those near his own residence and sending reliable 7 officers to do the same for those based further away. Where com- manders of garrisons and regiments and satraps are found to have the specified quota and to parade them equipped with excellent horses and arms, he promotes them on his honours list and rewards them with valuable gifts; but if he discovers commanders who have been neglecting their garrisons or making a profit out of them, he punishes them severely, relieves them of their command, and appoints others in their place. These actions would suggest to us that he shows an incontrovertible interest in military affairs. Moreover, he personally 8 inspects all of his territory that he sees as he travels through it, and what he does not see for himself he finds out by dispatching reliable commissioners. Where he can see that governors maintain their prov- ince well populated and their land efficiently cultivated and stocked with trees and crops indigenous to the region, he awards them more territory, loads them with presents, and rewards them with seats of honour; but wherever he finds land that is uncultivated and sparsely populated as a result of harsh rule or arrogance or neglect, he pun- ishes the governor, relieves him of his office, and appoints another in his place. Do you think these actions of his show he cares* less that his 9 land is well cultivated by its inhabitants than that it is properly pro- tected by its garrisons? There are officials charged by him with both duties, though not the same people: one group governs the inhabit- ants and workers and collects tribute from them, while the other com- mands armed men and garrisons. If a garrison commander provides 10 inadequate protection for the land, the civil governor, being responsible for agriculture, denounces him on the grounds that the land cannot be worked when it is not protected. Conversely, if a commander secures peaceful conditions for agriculture but the civil governor allows the population to decline and the land to become uncultivated, the commander in turn denounces him. It is broadly true that where

11 people cultivate the land inefficiently they are unable either to support garrisons or to pay tribute. Wherever a satrap is installed, he takes care of both these areas.

12   Here Critobulus said: Well, Socrates, if this is really what the King does, it seems to me that he pays as much attention to farming as he does to military matters.

13   Yes, and what is more, in all the places he resides and spends time, he ensures that there are so-called paradises, full of all the beautiful and useful plants that the earth brings forth. It is in these that he takes especial care to spend most of his time, except when the season of the year prevents it.

14   Good heavens, Socrates; if the King spends time in them, it must follow that these paradises will be exceptionably well maintained with trees and all other beautiful plants that the earth produces!

15   Some people say, Critobulus, that when the King is giving out presents the first people he summons are those who have distinguished themselves in war, on the grounds that there is no point in having large areas under cultivation if there is no one to protect them. After this he invites those who have looked after their lands best and kept them fertile, saying that even courageous men cannot live if there is

16 no one to till the soil. There is a story that Cyrus, that most celebrated King,* once remarked to those he had summoned to receive gifts that he himself deserved* to be awarded the presents given to both groups; for, as he said, 'I am the best at cultivating the land and the best at protecting it when it is cultivated.'

17   Well, Socrates, said Critobulus, if Cyrus said this, he prided himself as much on cultivating the land and keeping it productive as on his skill in warfare.

18   Assuredly so. If Cyrus* had only lived, he would have turned out to be a very fine ruler. There is a great deal of evidence* for this, including the fact that when he was on his way to fight his brother for the throne* not one man is said to have deserted from him to the

19 King, whereas tens of thousands did so the other way. I consider that this too is strong proof of a ruler's excellence, that men obey him willingly* and are prepared to stand by him in times of danger. His friends all fought at his side as long as Cyrus was alive, and after he

was killed died fighting around his body, except for Ariaeus, who happened to be stationed on the left wing. It was this Cyrus who, it is 20 said, treated Lysander* with great civility when he came to him bringing gifts from the allies. Lysander himself told the story to a guest-friend of his at Megara, adding that Cyrus had personally shown him round his paradise at Sardis. Lysander expressed admiration 21 for the beauty of the trees and the equal spacing between them, the straightness of their lines and the accuracy of the angles between them, as well as the many agreeable scents that accompanied them as they strolled, and said in wonder: 'Cyrus, I am astounded at the beauty of all this, but I admire even more the person who measured it out for you and aligned each of the trees so precisely.'

Hearing this Cyrus was delighted, and said, 'Well, Lysander, it 22 was I who measured everything and aligned it all—and some of the trees I actually planted myself.' Lysander related that he looked at 23 Cyrus, noting the elegance of the clothes he was wearing and their perfume, and the beauty of his necklets and bracelets and other ornaments,* and said, 'What are you saying, Cyrus? Did you really plant some of these with your own hand?' And it is said that Cyrus 24 replied, 'Does this surprise you, Lysander? I swear to you by Mithras that when I am in good health I never sit down to dinner until I have raised a sweat in some military or agricultural activity, or by taking part in some kind of competition.' Lysander himself 25 added that, on hearing this, he congratulated Cyrus and said, 'I believe you deserve your prosperity,* Cyrus; it is your virtue* that makes it happen.'

V

I TELL you this story, Critobulus, to show that even the most prosperous of men cannot manage without farming; for taking it seriously* seems to be at the same time an agreeable thing to do, a means of enlarging one's estate, and physical exercise leading to proficiency in all that is expected of a freeborn man. In the first place, for those who 2 cultivate it the earth produces what they need to live as well as good things for them to enjoy.

Secondly, it yields not only the means for them to adorn altars and 3 statues and themselves, but also the most pleasing sights and scents.

And, thirdly, there are luxury foods, which it either produces or else nurtures; for the art of managing livestock is a part of farming, so that men have enough to propitiate the gods with sacrificial victims and also animals for their own use.

4   And though the earth does provide an abundance of good things it does not let us take them without effort, but disciplines us to endure cold in winter and heat in summer. Through exercise it develops the physical strength of men who work with their hands and encourages manliness in their supervisors by rousing them early and forcing them to go about their work with energy; as we know, both on a farm

5 and in a city the most important jobs all have their fixed times. Then, again, if a man wants to serve his country* in the cavalry, farming is his ideal partner in maintaining a horse; and if he wants to join the infantry, farming keeps his body tough. The land also encourages him to develop an enthusiasm for the toil of hunting, for it provides

6 a ready supply of food for hounds as well as sustaining wild game. Horses and dogs may benefit from farming, but they benefit the farm in return: the horse by carrying its master to his duties and enabling him to return late, the hounds by keeping wild beasts from harming

7 crops and livestock, and also by providing security in remote places. The land also gives farmers an incentive to protect their country by force of arms, since the crops it produces are in open ground and so exposed to seizure by the strongest.

8   What occupation* makes men fitter for running, throwing, and leaping than farming? What occupation offers its practitioner a more generous return?* What occupation welcomes its follower* more cordially, with an invitation to come and take what he wants?

9 What occupation entertains guests more lavishly? Where can you spend winter more agreeably, with generous fires and warm baths, than on a farm? Where is it more pleasant to pass the summer, enjoying its running waters, breezes, and shade, than in the coun-

10 tryside? What occupation supplies more appropriate first fruits for the gods or encourages more plentiful festivals?* What occupation is more appreciated by slaves, more pleasing to one's wife, more

11 appealing to children,* more gratifying to friends? For my part, I should be very surprised if a freeborn man has ever owned anything that gives more pleasure than a farm, or has come across a more enjoyable activity or one more useful for making his livelihood than farming.

And besides, land is a goddess who teaches justice* to those who 12
are capable of learning from her, since those who serve her best are
given the best reward in return. And, if it ever happens that men who
are engaged in farming and so undergoing a tough and manly train- 13
ing are obliged by great armies to abandon their lands, they are well
equipped in mind and body—unless some god prevents it—to invade
the territory of those who are keeping them from their own and to
carry off the means of sustaining themselves. In wartime it is actually
often safer to go looking for food with weapons than to gather it with
agricultural implements.

Moreover, farming trains men to help each other. Just as in an 14
attack on the enemy you need others with you, so cultivation of the
land demands cooperation. The man who intends to farm efficiently 15
must engage labourers who are both eager for the task and prepared
to obey; and he who leads men against an enemy must devise a similar
system, rewarding the good soldiers who obey orders and punishing 16
the undisciplined. Often it is no less necessary for a farmer to encourage his workmen than a general his soldiers; slaves too need the hope
of good things ahead—more so, indeed, than free men, to make them
willing to stay.* It is a good saying that farming is the mother and
nurse of all occupations; for, when farming flourishes, all the other 17
arts prosper, but when the land is forced to lie unproductive, all other
arts on land and sea are virtually extinguished.

After hearing this Critobulus said: 18

Well, Socrates, I think you are right in what you have said so far.
But it's also true that in farming there are very many things that are
impossible to foresee: sometimes hail, frost, drought, rainstorms,
blight, and other disasters sweep away whatever has been well planned
and executed, and sometimes the best raised cattle are killed off by
disease in the most horrible way.

Yes; but I thought you knew, Critobulus, that in agriculture no 19
less than in war our affairs are controlled by the gods. You are aware,
I think, that in wartime men seek to propitiate the gods before an
engagement and ask them with the help of sacrifices and bird-omens
what they have to do and what to avoid. Do you suppose it is any less 20
necessary to seek the gods' good will when it comes to farming? You
may be sure that prudent farmers pray to the gods for fruits and
crops and cattle and horses and sheep, and indeed for all their
possessions.

VI

WELL, Socrates, said Critobulus, I think you are certainly right to tell us to get the gods on our side before any undertaking, seeing that they preside over peacetime activities no less than military ones. So we shall try to do just that. But now I'd like you to pick up from the point where you left off talking about estate management, and follow this topic, in detail, to its conclusion. After hearing what you said, I believe I have a better perception than before of what I must do to make a living.

2   Very well. What if we were to revisit the specific points we agreed on in our discussion, and then tried our best to reach a similar agreement* as we go through the remaining questions?

3   Certainly. Partners in financial matters are pleased if they can go through their accounts without arguing, and so should we, as partners in a discussion, if we can find agreement as we go through its next stages.

4   Well, said Socrates, this is what we agreed: that estate management is the name of a branch of knowledge, and this knowledge seems to be that by which men enlarge their estates. An estate was defined as the sum total of a person's property, and we said that property is what is useful* for making a living; and by useful we meant everything that

5 one knows how to use. We thought that it is impossible to learn every branch of knowledge, and agreed to disregard, as cities do, the so-called banausic occupations on the grounds that they seem to break

6 bodies down and destroy minds.* The plainest evidence for this, we said, was that, if during an enemy invasion we were to separate farmers from craftsmen and ask each group whether they would choose to

7 defend their land or to abandon it and guard their city walls, we thought that those whose business was with the land would vote to defend it, whereas craftsmen would not fight, preferring, in accord-

8 ance with their upbringing, to sit idly by and avoid exertion or danger. We reckoned that for a gentleman the best kind of work and branch of

9 knowledge was farming, from which men supply life's necessities. This was, we thought, very easy to learn and most agreeable to practise; it made one's body very handsome and strong, and provided the mind with plenty of time to cultivate the interests of friends and city. Because farming—growing crops and raising cattle—takes place

outside the city walls, we thought it acted as a kind of stimulant to 10
bravery in those who practised it. For these reasons we considered
this way of life to be highly regarded in our cities, since it produces
excellent citizens with a strong sense of service to the common good.

I think I am more than adequately persuaded, Socrates, that the 11
farmer's life is the finest, the most honourable, and the most agreeable* there is. Now, however, I should like to go back to what you said
before, that you have discovered why some people farm their land in
such a way as to produce an abundance of what they need, while others' management results in them making no profit. I should like to
hear the reasons for both cases, so that we may follow the good course
and avoid the harmful.

In that case, Critobulus, I have a proposal: to give you a full account 12
of a meeting I once had with a man who in my opinion was a genuine
member of that class we justly term gentlemen.*

I should very much like to hear it, seeing that it is my desire to
prove worthy of that title.

Very well, said Socrates, I'll tell you how I came to interview him. 13
It didn't take me long to make the round of good builders, good
bronze-smiths, good painters, good statue-makers, and suchlike, and
to examine those of their works that had a reputation for being beautiful. But then my soul had a great desire to investigate those who 14
enjoyed the respected title of gentleman* and to find out what they
did to deserve it. To begin with, because the epithet 'beautiful' is 15
attached to 'good' in this word, whenever I saw a beautiful man
I would approach him and see if I could discover if his beauty had any
goodness attached to it. But it didn't turn out as I expected. I found 16
that some men of beautiful appearance in fact had very depraved
souls. So I thought I should give up beauty and look for someone with
a reputation for being 'beautiful and good', that is, a gentleman. I was 17
told that Ischomachus* was universally held to deserve that name, in
the opinion of women as well as men, foreigners as well as citizens,*
so I thought I should try to arrange a meeting with him.

VII

So, catching sight of him one day sitting in the stoa of Zeus Eleutherios,*
apparently with nothing to do, I went over and sat beside him and said:

'What's going on, Ischomachus? It's not like you to sit around doing nothing. Usually when I see you in the agora* you're busy with something, or at any rate not totally idle.'

2   'And you wouldn't be seeing me unoccupied now, Socrates, if I hadn't arranged to meet some guests* here.'

'I see; but tell me, where do you spend your time and what do you do when you're not tied up with something like this? I'd very much like to know what it is you do that leads people to call you a gentleman, since you clearly don't pass your time indoors, and your physical condition is obviously not that of someone who does.'

3   Ischomachus laughed at my asking what he did to be called a gentleman; he was I think gratified by it, and said:

'I don't know why some people give me that name when they talk with you. When they challenge me to a property exchange concerning payment for a trireme or a dramatic chorus* they certainly don't go looking for a gentleman, but simply refer to me as Ischomachus, adding my father's name. As to your question, Socrates, no, I definitely don't live indoors; my wife* is more than capable of managing our domestic affairs on her own.'*

4   'Ah, now that is what I would particularly like to hear from you—whether you personally trained your wife in her duties, or if she already knew how to manage a household when you received her from her father and mother.'

5   'What could she have known, Socrates, when I married her? She was not 15 when she came to me, and up to that time had lived
6 under strict supervision, which meant that she saw, heard, and spoke as little as possible.* If all she knew when she came was how to take wool and make a cloak, and had seen how spinning tasks were allocated to slaves, don't you think that was the sum of what I could expect? And she was also very well schooled in controlling her appetite, which I consider an important discipline in both men and women.'*

7   'But did you train* your wife yourself, Ischomachus, in other respects as well, so that she was competent to carry out her duties?'*

8   'Of course not—at least not until I'd made a sacrifice and prayed for my success in teaching and hers in learning what was best for us both.'

'And did your wife make exactly the same sacrifice and prayers as you?'

'Indeed she did. She promised and prayed earnestly to the gods to become the kind of woman she ought to be, and it was quite clear she would not neglect what she'd been taught.'

'Well, well!' I said. 'Tell me what was the first lesson you taught 9 her. I'd much rather hear this from you than a description of even the most brilliant* athletic contest or horse race!'

'Very well, Socrates. As soon as she was tamed and sufficiently 10 domesticated* to carry on a conversation,* I questioned her along these lines: "Have you worked out, wife, why I married you and why your parents gave you to me? It must I think be obvious to you as well 11 that there was no lack of potential sleeping partners for either of us; but I on my behalf, and your parents on yours, thought about who would be the best person to take a share in* both household and children, and out of those who were acceptable I chose you and your parents apparently chose me. Now, if ever the god grants us children, 12 we shall have to decide how best to educate them. This too will be a shared blessing for us, for we shall find in them the best of allies and supporters in our old age; but now of course all that we have in com- 13 mon is this estate. I continue to pay everything I possess into our common fund, and you have deposited there all that you brought with you. We do not need to calculate exactly which of us has put more into it, though we should be quite clear that the one who turns out to be the better partner is the one who makes the more valuable contribution."*

In reply, my wife said: "How can I possibly be an equal partner 14 with you? What power do I have? Everything here is under your control. My only duty, according to my mother, is to practise self-control."*

"Quite right, wife," I said; "and in fact my father said the same to 15 me. But self-control, you know, for both husband and wife means maintaining one's property in the best possible state and adding to it as much as you can in an honest and fair way."

"And what do you think I could possibly do", said my wife, "to 16 enlarge our estate?"

"In heaven's name," I said, "all you have to do is to try as hard as you can to do exactly what the gods have fitted you* to do and the law approves."

"And what is that?"   17

"Something in no way trivial, in my opinion—unless of course you think the tasks which the queen bee presides over in a hive are of little

18 significance. It seems to me that the gods have shown great perception in yoking male and female, as they are termed, so as to constitute
19 a most mutually beneficial partnership.* In the first place, so that the
race of living beings may not die out, the pair lies together for the
purpose of producing children; and in the second, it means that from
this union human beings at any rate will have children to look after
them in their old age. Thirdly, unlike cattle, humans do not live in the
20 open air, but obviously need shelter. However, those who intend to
grow crops to store under cover also need people to work outside:
ploughing, sowing, planting, and herding are all jobs carried out in
21 the open air, and it is from these that life's necessities are secured.
Then again, when this produce is brought under cover, there is a need
for someone to look after it, and to do what has to be done indoors.
Looking after newborn children also requires shelter, as does turning
22 grain into bread and wool into clothes. And, as both these activities,
indoor and outdoor, demand work and care,* it seems to me that the
god has from the beginning accommodated women's nature to indoor
23 tasks and responsibilities and men's to those out of doors. Men's bodies he shaped to be better able to bear cold, heat, travel, and military
service, and so assigned them outdoor activities, but, because he made
24 women's bodies less tolerant of these, he allotted them, I believe,
indoor tasks. But, knowing he had instilled in woman, and prescribed
for her, nurture of the newborn, he also gave to her a greater share of
25 love for babies than to man. And, because he had assigned to woman
the job of looking after what is brought into the house, being aware
that for a guardian a timid disposition is no drawback, he awarded her
a greater portion of fear than to man. He also knew that the one
26 who works outdoors will also need to act as their defender against
wrongdoers, and so gave man a greater share of courage. But, since
both have also to give and take,* he apportioned memory and concern* even-handedly to both, so that you could not differentiate
27 between male and female as to who has the greater part* of these
qualities. Self-control* too the god has distributed impartially to
both, and has determined that whichever of them, man or woman,
shows greater aptitude in this shall enjoy more of the benefit which
28 flows from it. However, since neither is naturally endowed with all
these aptitudes, they have all the more need for each other, and the
29 pairing is the more beneficial to both when one member is able to
make up for the deficiencies in the other. Bearing in mind, wife,"

I said, "what the god has dispensed to each of us, we must both do our ₃₀ best to carry out our separate duties. The law supports this, by join-ing man and wife together: it makes them partners not only in raising children but also in their household. The law also states that those duties are honourable for which the god has made one naturally* more competent than the other. It is more honourable for a woman to stay indoors than to wander abroad, while for a man it is more shameful to ₃₁ stay at home than to busy himself with outdoor matters. Those who go against the nature that the god has implanted in them may well be seen as upsetting the divine order of things, and will be punished for ₃₂ neglecting their own affairs or interfering in their wives'. It seems to me," I said, "that this is the kind of work, laid down by the gods, that the queen bee* is constantly engrossed in."*

"What duties," she said, "does the queen bee have that are similar to mine?"

"Well, she stays in the hive and makes sure the bees aren't idle, she ₃₃ dispatches those who have work to do outside, she knows and takes charge of what each bee brings back and stores it until it is time to use it, and when that time arrives she allots each bee its fair share.* She ₃₄ oversees the fabrication of combs in the hive, making sure they are quickly and skilfully made, and concerns herself with the upbringing of the new brood; and, when the young bees are grown up and ready for work, she sends them out to found a colony, with a leader to guide the new generation."

"Good heavens," said my wife, "shall I have to do all this?" ₃₅

"Most certainly," I said. "You will have to stay at home and dis-patch gangs of slaves* who have work outside, and supervise those ₃₆ with indoor jobs. You must take charge of whatever is brought into the house, and release whatever part of it has to be spent, while taking thought for* any surplus and keeping that safe, so that what should suffice for a year is not spent in one month. When wool is brought home, you must see to it that clothes are made for those who need them; and you must take care that the dry grain is in good condition ₃₇ for turning into food. There is, however, one duty that you may find disagreeable: you must ensure that any slave who falls ill is well looked after."

"On the contrary!" said my wife. "It will be a most agreeable task, if it means that whoever is well cared for will be grateful to me, and more loyal than before."*

38   Ischomachus said "I was delighted with this answer", and said to her: "Is it not the case, wife, that it is this kind of considerate attitude that means the other bees are so faithful to the queen, so that when she abandons the hive not one of them thinks of deserting, but all follow her?"

39   My wife replied: "I should be surprised if the leader's responsibilities did not apply to you rather than to me, for my guardianship and management of the house's contents would appear ridiculous if you did not make sure that supplies were being brought into it from outside."

40   "On the other hand," I said, "my bringing things in would seem equally absurd if there was no one there to look after them. You must know the saying, that those who draw water in a vessel full of holes are to be pitied, because their labour seems to be pointless?"

      "Yes, of course; they are clearly in a bad way if this is indeed what they do."

41   "Still," I said, "I can tell you that some of your other duties will turn out to be pleasurable: for example, when you take on a slave who doesn't know how to spin and teach her that skill, and so double her value to you; or when you take on someone who knows nothing about housekeeping or service and turn her into a skilled and trustworthy

42   servant, thus increasing her value considerably; or when it is in your power to reward self-disciplined and helpful slaves in your house and to punish the lazy. Your greatest pleasure, however, will be if you are seen to be better than me, and can make me your servant.* You will have no fear as you grow older of becoming less respected in your own house; rather, you will be confident as the years pass that the better partner you prove to me and the better guardian of the estate for our

43   children, the more honoured you will be in the household. It is not because of youthful attractiveness that what is good and beautiful* multiplies in human lives, but through the exercise of virtues.'*

      'I believe these were the kind of topics, Socrates, that I first discussed with my wife, as far as I remember them.'

VIII

'AND did you notice, Ischomachus, that this conversation stimulated your wife to be more diligent?'*

'It certainly did. At any rate, one day I saw that she was looking irritated, and blushed deeply because she couldn't give me something that was stored in the house when I asked her for it. Seeing her ₂ distress* I said, "Don't be cast down, wife, because you can't give me what I asked for. Not to have something when you need it is the essence of poverty; but to look for something and be unable to find it is a less grievous kind of need than not to seek it in the first place because you know it's not there. No, it's not your fault but mine for not instructing you where to store each article when I gave it to you, so you would know where to put it and where to find it again. There is ₃ nothing so helpful or so satisfactory* for human beings as order.* Take choruses:* a chorus is made up of people, but if everyone acts as he fancies chaos ensues, and it gives the spectators no pleasure, while when they move and sing in an orderly way the same people are well ₄ worth watching and listening to. Or there's an army: when it lacks discipline it is a total shambles, an easy target for enemies, utterly use-less to its allies, and a shameful spectacle—a jumble of donkeys, hop-lites, baggage-carriers, light-armed infantry, cavalry, and carts. How are they to move forward, if they are going to get in each other's way, the slow-moving obstructing those running and runners impeding those standing still, carts in the path of cavalry, donkeys in the way of carts, ₅ baggage-carriers obstructing hoplites? If fighting has to be done, how can they fight in a state like this, for those who are forced to run away before an advancing enemy are ideally placed to trample under- ₆ foot men who still have their arms. But an army drawn up in good order is a splendid sight to its allies, and a very tough prospect for its opponents. What ally would not be delighted to see a mass of hoplites advancing in order? Who would not admire cavalry riding in squad-rons? What enemy would not be terrified at the sight of hoplites, cav-alry, light-armed men, archers, and slingers separately organized and following their officers in good order? When soldiers march in order, ₇ even if they number tens of thousands, they all move smoothly as one man, because each man constantly fills up the space left empty in ₈ front of him. Then again, why is a heavily manned trireme a source of terror to enemies and a pleasing sight to allies, if not because of its speed? Must it not be that the crew do not obstruct each other because they sit, swing forward, and pull back in order, and board and disem-bark in order as well? A roughly similar example of disorder would in ₉ my view be a farmer dumping barley, wheat, and beans all in one bin,

and then when he needed a barley-cake, bread, or a side dish, having
10 to pick through the heap instead of finding them carefully separated
for his use. Now, wife, if you wish to avoid this kind of chaos, to
understand exactly how to manage our property, to find with ease
whatever we need to use, and to please me by giving me anything I ask
for, let us determine the appropriate place for each item and instruct
the maid to take it from there and put it back in the same place. In this
way we shall know what is safely stored and what is not, because the
place itself will miss what is not there, and a quick look will tell us
what needs attention, and the knowledge of where each thing is will
11 soon put it in our hands, so that we shall never be unable to use it."

I think that the most elegant arrangement of tackle I ever saw,
Socrates, was when I once went on board that huge Phoenician merchant ship* to have a look over it. What I saw was an enormous range
of objects stowed separately in a very small space. You may know that
12 a vessel is steered into harbour and puts to sea again by means of a lot
of wooden gear and ropes, and uses a great deal of rigging—as it is
called—when it sails. It is equipped with many devices to defend it
against enemy ships, it carries on its voyages many weapons for the
crew, and transports the same pots and pans that men use for each
shared meal as they do at home. As well as all this, it is loaded with the
13 cargo that ship captains carry for profit. Everything I am talking
about could be fitted into the space not much larger than a ten-couch
dining room.* I noticed that every item was stored in such a way as
not to interfere with another; they needed no one to look for them,
were perfectly ready for use, and were not difficult to unlash, which
14 could cause delay when rapid use was required. I found that the
helmsman's assistant, called the bowman, knew the exact location of
everything, could tell you where each item was stowed and how many
of them there were even when he couldn't see them; just like someone
who knows his alphabet can tell you the number of letters in Socrates'
15 name and what order they come in. I saw this man', said Ischomachus,
'using his spare time to check thoroughly all the tackle that might be
needed on the voyage. I was surprised at this close scrutiny and asked
him what he was doing. "My friend," he said, "I am inspecting the
contents of the ship to see where everything is stowed, in case an
16 emergency arises or if anything is missing, or if it is in the wrong
place. When the god sends us a storm at sea, there is no time to look
for what you need or to hand it out if things are in a mess. The god,

you see, threatens and punishes the slipshod. One must be content if he simply stops short of destroying the innocent; and if he spares those who do their job efficiently, well, we should give him heartfelt thanks." So, having observed how methodically his gear was arranged, 17 I said to my wife, "If mariners in merchant ships, even small ones, can find room for things, and keep good order even when violently storm-tossed, and know where to find what they need even when panic-stricken, it would be extremely slovenly of us, who have large separate storerooms in a house that rests on firm ground, not to find good and easily identifiable places for everything. Would that not be 18 the height of stupidity on our part? I have already demonstrated what a good thing it is to have one's possessions arranged in proper order, and how useful it is in a house to find an appropriate place for 19 each item. And what a beautiful sight it is to see shoes of different kinds organized in rows, and garments of different kinds in their proper places, and bedclothes, bronze ware, and tableware! And—something a serious man might not find very funny but a frivolous man would—I maintain that pots and pans look graceful when grouped in a discriminating way. It follows that all other 20 things too somehow appear more beautiful when arranged in order; for each collection looks like a chorus* of objects, and the space between them is a beautiful sight, when each one stands clear of the rest, just as a cyclic chorus is not only beautiful in itself but the empty space looks beautiful and uncluttered. We can test the truth 21 of what I say, wife, without inconvenience and without putting ourselves out greatly. Moreover, we must not be disheartened by the thought that it is hard to find someone capable of learning the correct places and who can remember to put each item back where it 22 belongs. We surely know that the city in its entirety contains many thousand times the sum of our property, and yet not one of the slaves you send to buy something in the agora and bring it home will be unsure what to do. They will all know where to go to buy each item, and the reason is that everything will be in its designated 23 place. If, on the other hand, you are looking for a person, you may often abandon the search, even if he is also looking for you—the only reason being, once again, that it has not been decided where each person has to wait."

'As I recollect, this was the drift of the conversation I had with my wife about the disposition and use of articles.'*

IX

'AND what happened next, Ischomachus?' I said. 'Did your wife seem to go along with any of the lessons you were keen to teach her?'

'Of course. She promised to give them her attention and was obviously deeply pleased at having found a way out of a perplexing situation. She asked me to lose no time in setting things up in the way I had described.'

2 'And how did you do that?'

'Well, the first thing was clearly to explain the house's possibilities to her. It has no painted decoration, Socrates, but its rooms were constructed specifically to serve as receptacles for what was to be stored
3 in them, so that each room invited what was appropriate to it. Thus the bedroom, because of its strong position, invited the most expensive bedding and furniture, while dry storerooms called for grain, cool ones for wine, and well-lit areas for things that needed light, like
4 textiles and utensils. I showed her the family's decorated living rooms that were cool in summer and warm in winter. I explained how the whole house faces south, so that it enjoys sun in winter and shade in
5 summer. I pointed out the women's quarters* as well, separated by a bolted door from the men's area, the point being that nothing unauthorized should be removed from them, and that slaves should be prevented from breeding without our permission. (Good slaves are generally more loyal when they have produced children, but when
6 bad ones mate they are more inclined to become troublemakers.) When we had gone through all this, we set about sorting our portable property by category. We began by assembling what we use at sacrifices, and then separated out women's holiday finery and men's clothing for festivals and war; then bedding in both women's and men's quarters, and women's and men's shoes. There was one category for
7 weapons, others for implements used in spinning, bread-making, and cooking, and others for bathing, kneading, and for use at table. All
8 these we divided into two groups, one for everyday and one for festival use. We also put aside what was to be consumed within a month and what was calculated to last a year; in this way we were less likely to misjudge how things will turn out at the year's end. When we had
9 sorted out all our portable property by category we put each item in its appropriate place. After this we indicated to the slaves where they

were to keep the utensils they use every day, such as for baking, cooking, spinning, or similar, and handed these over, with orders to keep them safe. As for the articles we use on feast days or for entertaining 10 guests or only from time to time, we entrusted them to the housekeeper; we showed her each one's place, counted and listed them, and told her to issue what each slave needed, but to remember what she had given to each, and after getting it back to replace it where she had 11 found it.

When we appointed our housekeeper, we looked for the one whom we judged to have the best control over her appetite for food and drink, and her need for sleep and the company of men; and also who seemed to have the best memory, and to be keen to avoid punishment by us for neglecting her duties, and to look for ways of earning 12 a reward* by doing things that pleased us. We also trained her to be loyal to us by sharing with her any occasion we had for rejoicing and also taking her into our confidence in times of trouble. We encouraged in her a desire to improve our estate, by familiarizing her with it and by giving her a share in its prosperity. And we instilled in her 13 a sense of justice by the way we valued just people above unjust, and by showing that they lived lives of greater wealth and freedom. And so we appointed her to this position. 14

In addition to all this, Socrates, I told my wife that there would be no point in making all these dispositions if she did not herself ensure that they were maintained in every respect. I explained* to her that in the best conducted cities it wasn't enough for the citizens to pass good laws but that they should appoint guardians for them, who as part of their oversight should commend lawful behaviour and punish 15 transgression. So I told my wife to regard herself as guardian of the laws of the house, and to inspect its equipment when she thought it appropriate, just as a garrison commander inspects his guards; and, just as the Council* checks its horses and cavalry, she should check that every single thing is in good order, and, like a queen,* should praise and honour to the best of her ability all those who deserve it and hand out censure and punishment to those who fall short. 16 Moreover, I made her see that she would have no reason to be upset if I gave her more responsibility than the slaves as concerned our possessions, pointing out that slaves' interest in their master's property is limited to carrying, looking after, and guarding it, and that none of them has the right to use anything without their master's permission; 17

everything belongs to the master, to use in any way he chooses. I explained that he who stands to benefit most from the preservation of property and to suffer most from its damage has the greatest interest in looking after it.'

18   'Well, Ischomachus,' I said, 'was you wife minded to listen to you when she heard all this?'

'In fact, Socrates, she actually said to me that I was mistaken* if I thought I was giving her a hard job in telling her she had to look after our property. She said it would have been harder if I had instructed her to neglect her possessions rather than to be obliged to

19   take care of them. "For just as it seems more natural", she said, "for a sensible woman to care for her children than to neglect them, so such a person will find it more satisfying to look after her possessions than to neglect them, inasmuch as they belong to her".'

X

WHEN I heard the answer his wife gave, I said, 'Well, I declare, Ischomachus, you're telling me your wife thinks like a man!'*

'Yes', he said, 'and I'd like to give you some more examples of her high-mindedness, when I only had to say a word to gain instant obedience.'*

'Do tell me about them,' I said. 'It would give me far more pleasure to hear of a living woman's virtues than if Zeuxis* showed me a portrait he'd painted of a beautiful one.'

2   Ischomachus continued: 'One day I noticed that she had worked a lot of white powder* into her face, to make herself look whiter than she was, and a lot of rouge, to make her complexion look rosier than it

3   really was; and she was wearing high-soled shoes to increase her natural stature. "Tell me," I said, "would you judge me more worthy of your love as a partner in our wealth if I revealed the true state of our possessions to you, and didn't boast that I own more than I actually do, and didn't hide any part of them from you; or if I tried to deceive you, exaggerating their extent, by showing you counterfeit money,

4   wooden necklaces painted gold, and purple clothes whose dye was fading, claiming they were genuine?" She immediately replied, "Hush—don't ever say such a thing! I wouldn't be able to love you with all my heart if you said that."

"And were we not joined in union as partners of each other's bodies?"

"Well, that's what people say, at any rate."

"So how should I seem to be more deserving of your love* in this partnership? By trying to keep my body fit and strong, and so presenting to you a genuinely healthy complexion, or making deceitful love to you daubed with rouge and painted with eye make-up, offering you the sight and touch of rouge instead of my natural skin?" 5

"Speaking for myself," she said, "I would much rather touch you than rouge and look at your true colour than at make-up, and see your eyes in their healthy condition than painted with cosmetics." 6

Ischomachus told me he said to her, "You should therefore bear in mind, wife, that I too take more pleasure in your true colour than in white lead and alkanet.* Just as the gods have designed horses to delight in horses, and cattle and sheep likewise, so men take most pleasure in an unadorned human body. Deceits like these may perhaps mislead strangers without being detected, but if people who live together try to deceive one another they will inevitably be found out. They are found out when they are getting up from bed before dressing, or they are given away by sweat or tears, or when shown as they really are when taking a bath." 7 8

'Good heavens,' I said. 'What did she say to that?' 9

'Naturally, she never got up to such tricks* again, but tried to present herself in a natural and seemly manner. She did, however, ask me if I could advise her how to make herself truly beautiful instead of simply appearing to be so. So I urged her not to sit around all the time like a slave, but—with the gods' help—to make the effort to stand at her loom as a mistress of the house should, to be prepared to teach others what she knew better than them, and to learn anything* she did not know so well; to supervise the slave who makes bread, to stand next to the housekeeper when she is measuring out goods, and to walk about the house and check whether everything is in its proper place. I thought that this would give her an opportunity for exercise as well as the chance to carry out her duties. Wetting and kneading bread was good physical training, I said, as was folding and shaking out clothing and bed linen. Exercise would give her a better appetite, better health, and a genuinely better complexion. Moreover, when a wife's appearance overshadows that of a slave, and she is unadorned and becomingly dressed, it is sexually attractive,* especially when she is also 10 11 12

willing to please, whereas a slave-girl* is compelled to do what a man
13 wants. Those wives, on the other hand, who spend all their time sitting around looking grand lay themselves open to comparison with
women who aim to deceive by the use of make-up. And now, Socrates,
you may be sure that my wife orders her life in the way I have taught
her,* and as I have just told you.'

XI

I THEN said, 'I think I have heard enough, Ischomachus, about your
wife's affairs* for now; and it reflects very well on both of you. But
now it's your turn to tell me about your own business, which means
that you will enjoy relating the reasons for your good reputation, and
I will be deeply grateful for hearing a full account of a gentleman's
conduct, and—so far as I can—absorbing it.'

2   'Of course,' he said. 'It will give me great pleasure to describe what
I do day by day; and you may put me right if you think I am wrong in
anything I do.'

3   'As to that,' I said, 'who am I to correct someone who is a perfect
gentleman,* especially when I have a reputation as an idle prattler
and an air-measurer,* and am also called poverty-stricken*—which
4 I consider a really stupid accusation. This last charge would in fact
have upset me greatly, had I not the other day come across the horse
that belongs to Nicias* the foreigner. I saw there was a crowd following and staring at it and heard people talking at length about it. So
I went up to the groom and asked him if the horse owned many pos-
5 sessions. He looked at me as if I was out of my mind and said, "How
can a horse own property?" This cheered me up, as it was evidently
acceptable for even a poor horse to be a good one, if it had a naturally
6 good spirit. So it is also right and proper for me too to become a good
man. Accordingly, give me a full account of your activities, so that
I may listen and learn to the best of my ability, and try to imitate you.
I can start tomorrow, for that, they say, is a good day to set out on
a course of excellence.'*

7   'You're making fun of me,' said Ischomachus. 'All the same, I'll
8 explain the principles that I have tried, to the best of my ability, to
follow throughout my life. I believe I have learnt that though the gods
do not regard it as right that men should prosper without knowing

their duties and making sure they are carried out, to some who are sensible and diligent they grant prosperity, and to others they deny it. I therefore begin by reverencing the gods; I try to act in a way that ensures that my prayers secure for me health and strength of body, a good reputation in the city, the goodwill of my friends, security with honour in war, and an honest increase in wealth.'

'Is it that important to you, Ischomachus, to be rich and have many 9 possessions when looking after them brings you a lot of problems?'

'The answer is that it certainly is,* because I consider it a pleasure to make lavish offerings to the gods, to help a friend in need, and to see that the city lacks no embellishment that I can pay for.'

'Well,' I said, 'these are fine sentiments you express, and worthy of 10 a truly powerful man. How can they not be, seeing that there are many men who can't live without asking others for help, and many who must put up with an existence at subsistence level. But those who are able not only to manage their own estates but also make enough surplus to embellish the city and lighten their friends' burdens must surely be regarded as men of affluence and power. We can all approve 11 of men like this; but I want you to go back to what you said first, and tell me how you look after your health and physical strength, and how it is right for you to survive with honour even in time of war. After that there will be time enough for me to hear how you make your money.'

'It seems to me, Socrates, that these things follow one on another. 12 When someone has enough to eat, and works it off by suitable exercise, I think health attaches itself to him, and the more he exercises the stronger he becomes. Taking part in military training means he is more likely to survive with honour, and if he applies himself and 13 avoids going soft the more likely he is to increase his estate.'

'I can follow you so far,' I said, 'when you say that by vigorous exercise, by application,* and by training a man is more likely to obtain the good things in life; but what I really want to know is the kind of exercise that leads to wellbeing and strength, how you train for fighting, and how you apply yourself to making a surplus in order to benefit your friends and the city.'

'Very well,' said Ischomachus, 'I'll tell you. My routine is to get up 14 at a time when if there's anyone I may want to see I can catch him at home. If I have any business in the city I use the opportunity this 15 presents to take a walk. If I have nothing pressing to do in the city, my

slave takes my horse to the farm, and I turn my journey there into
16 a walk, which is possibly better for me than a stroll in the arcade.
When I reach the farm, whether my men are planting, clearing the
ground, sowing, or harvesting, I inspect each activity carefully and
17 make changes if I know of any way they could do their job more efficiently. After this I generally mount my horse and practise, as far as
I can, the equestrian exercises closest to those essential in war. I do
not avoid hillsides or steep slopes or ditches or streams, though I do
18 my best not to lame my horse while he is engaged on these man-
oeuvres. This done, my slave gives the horse a roll and leads him
home, taking with him from the farm anything we may need in the
city. On my way home I walk and run by turns, and when I get there
I scrape myself down with a strigil. After this I have my lunch, eating
enough to get me through the day without feeling empty or too full.'

19 'I do find all this very satisfactory,' I said. 'To keep yourself busy
with activities designed to promote health and strength, with exercises to improve military skills, and with schemes to increase your
20 wealth, and all at the same time—this is in my view wholly admirable.
And in fact you give us plenty of proof of your competence in each of
these exercises, since we can see that, with the gods' help, you are
generally fit and healthy. And we know you are reckoned to be one of
the best horsemen and richest citizens here.'

21 'This is indeed the life I lead, Socrates, and yet a lot of people say
22 abusive things about me—though perhaps you thought I was going to
say that many people called me a gentleman.'

'I was actually going to ask if you were also interested in acquiring
the skill of prosecuting and defending, in case you had to appear in
court.'*

'Is it not obvious to you, Socrates, that I am constantly doing just
that—demonstrating that I do wrong to no man and good to as many
as I can? Don't you understand that it is my practice to act as a pros-
ecutor, when I observe that there are people who do wrong to many
private citizens and to the city but good to no one?'

23 'So please tell me if you also rehearse delivering speeches of
this kind.'

'I never stop practising the art of speaking,' he said. 'If one of my
slaves accuses another or is himself accused, I listen and try to cross-
examine him; or I praise or criticize someone to his friends; or I medi-
ate between acquaintances by trying to persuade them that it is more

in their interest to be friends than enemies; or we meet and pass cen- 24
sure on some general, or defend someone who has been wrongly
accused, or else take turns in accusing someone who has been unde-
servedly awarded an honour. We frequently deliberate among ourselves, speaking on behalf of the course we wish to follow and against
the one we disapprove of. In the past, Socrates, I have often been 25
singled out and sentenced to suffer some punishment or pay a fine.'

'By whom, Ischomachus? I had no idea this happened!'

'By my wife.'*

'And how do you defend yourself?'

'Pretty well when it suits me to speak the truth, but when it's
expedient to lie I'm utterly incapable of making the weaker case
appear the stronger.'*

'Perhaps, Ischomachus, it's because you can't turn falsehood into
truth.'

XII

'BUT I mustn't keep you,' I went on, 'and you may well want to get
away now.'

'Not at all, Socrates; I won't be leaving until the market finally
closes.'

'You are obviously very careful not to throw away that title of 2
gentleman,' I said; 'and, although there are probably many things that
require your attention now, you are still waiting for those guests you
agreed to meet, and you won't let them down.'

'But I assure you, Socrates, those matters you mention won't be
neglected, either; I have foremen on my land, you see.'

'When you have need of a foreman,* Ischomachus, do you find out 3
if there is anyone around with the necessary skills, and then try to buy
him, just as when you need a builder I'm sure you look for someone
with building skills and try to get hold of him? Or do you train your
foremen yourself?'

'Obviously, I try to train them myself. If the man is going to run my 4
affairs satisfactorily in my absence, can there be anything he needs to
know apart from what I know myself? If I'm capable of managing my
own farm, I must presumably be able to pass this knowledge on to
someone else.'

5   'In the first place, then, if he is going to deputize satisfactorily in your absence, he will have to be loyal to you and yours. Without loyalty, what is the use of any kind of knowledge that your foreman may possess?'

'None, of course, Socrates. Hence loyalty to me and mine is the first thing I try to instil.'

6   'But how on earth can you teach the man you've chosen loyalty to you and yours?'

'Needless to say, by giving him a share in any abundant good fortune the gods may grant us.'

7   'Are you saying that those who enjoy a share in your good things turn out to be loyal to you, and keen for you to prosper?'

'Indeed I am, Socrates. I regard this as the best tool for securing their loyalty.'

8   'And if someone is loyal to you, will he for that reason be qualified to act as your foreman? You know, of course, that, while all human beings are, so to speak, loyal to themselves, nevertheless there are many who are unwilling to make the effort to acquire the good things they desire.'

9   'Yes, of course; but when I wish to appoint such people as foremen, I also teach them how to apply themselves.'*

10   'How can you possibly do that?' I said. 'I always thought that application was completely unteachable.'

'True; it's certainly not possible to teach it to everyone you meet.'

11   'Well, what kind of people *can* you teach? Please tell me who they are.'

'To begin with, you can't teach application to people who can't handle wine, because drunkenness makes them forget everything they have to do.'

12   'So are drunkards the only people who can't be taught application? Or are there others?'

'There certainly are,' said Ischomachus. 'There are those who sleep too much. A sleeping man can neither carry out his own duties nor direct others to do theirs.'

13   'So will these be the only ones incapable of learning application, or are there others as well?'

'Yes, I believe there are. People in the grip of an infatuation can't be taught to concentrate on anything beyond it. It's not easy for

them to look forward to or occupy themselves with anything more
enjoyable than commitment to their boyfriends; nor indeed, when
they are under pressure to do something, can one think of a severer
punishment than barring them from the object of their desire.
Accordingly, I've given up even trying to turn people in whom I recognize these traits into responsible people.' 14

'What about those in love with profit? Are these too incapable of
being trained to take charge of a farm's business?' 15

'No, not at all. They can easily be induced to take it seriously, since
one has only to point out that applying oneself is profitable.'

'As to the rest,' I said, 'provided they can control themselves in
matters where you demand it, and keep their love of profit within
limits, how do you teach them to take an interest in those areas you
want them to?' 16

'It's perfectly simple, Socrates. When I see they are ready to be
involved, I praise them and try to award them some mark of honour;
but, if they lose interest, I try to say and do the kind of thing that will
hurt them.'

'Now, Ischomachus,' I said, 'I'd like you to turn our discussion
away from training people to show some application and explain the
training* itself. Is it possible for someone who lacks application to
encourage it in others?' 17

'Certainly not,' he said; 'You would as soon expect an artistically
untalented person to turn other people into artists. When a teacher
explains something badly, it is hard for the student to learn how to do
it well; and, if a master shows poor application, it is, of course, difficult for a slave to learn how to apply himself. In short, I don't think
I have ever encountered a bad master with good slaves. (I have come
across bad slaves belonging to a good master, but they've never
escaped punishment.) No, the man who wants to encourage application in his men must oversee and scrutinize their work, and be ready
to commend those who perform it well and not be afraid of handing
out appropriate punishment to the careless. I like that remark attributed to a foreigner,* I mean when his King* had found a good horse
and wanted to fatten it up as quickly as possible. So he asked someone
who had a reputation for being good with horses what was the quickest way to do this. It is said the man replied, "Its master's eye". And
so in general, Socrates, I think we may say that it is the master's eye
that produces the best and finest results.'* 18 19 20

XIII

'BUT once you have driven the lesson strongly into a man,' I said, 'that he must apply himself to whatever task you give him, will he then be capable of acting as a foreman, or is there something else he has to learn if he is going to do the job properly?'

2   'There certainly is,' said Ischomachus. 'It still remains for him to understand what the job is, and when he has to do it, and how. If he doesn't, he will be no more use as a foreman than a doctor who conscientiously visits a patient morning and evening but has no idea what the right kind of treatment for him is.'

3   'Very well; if he has learnt how farm work is to be done, is there anything else in your view he needs to do to become a thoroughly proficient foreman?'

'I think he must learn how to govern his workers.'

4   'So you also train your foremen to be competent governors?'

'Well, I do try,' said Ischomachus.

'And how, may I ask, do you train them to be governors of men?'

'It's very simple, Socrates—so simple that you may well laugh when I tell you.'

5   'This is no laughing matter, you know, Ischomachus. Anyone who can train people to be capable of governing others can clearly also train them to exercise mastery, and, if he can make men fit to be masters, he can also make them fit to be kings.* A man who can do this seems to me to deserve not ridicule but great praise.'

6   'Well, Socrates, other living things learn obedience in two ways:
7   from being punished when they try to disobey, and being rewarded when they serve willingly. Take colts: they learn obedience to their horse-breakers when they realize that submission brings a pleasant experience, and disobedience means trouble; and in the end they yield to their breaker's will.

8   Puppies, too, which are far inferior to men in intelligence and speech, learn to run in circles and turn somersaults and many other tricks in just the same way; for, when they are obedient, they get
9   something they want, while disobedience brings punishment. When it comes to humans, it is possible to make them more obedient through reason, by pointing out that it's in their interest to do what they're told. In the case of slaves, however, the most effective method of

obedience training is the one appropriate to beasts; if you indulge the
desires of their stomachs, you get much from them in return.
Ambitious natures are sharpened by praise, since some temperaments
are as hungry for praise as others are for food and drink. These are 10
the rules I myself follow in order to make people more tractable, and
I teach them to those whom I wish to appoint as foremen; and I support them in other ways as well: I take care that the clothes and shoes
I am obliged to provide for my workers are not all alike, but some are
better than others, so that the better workmen are rewarded with
superior clothing while the less proficient are given inferior stuff. It is 11
my view that good men become dispirited if they can see that, though
they actually do all the work, they receive the same reward as those
who are reluctant to work or to take risks when they need to. For 12
myself, I feel strongly that good workers should not receive the same
treatment as inferior ones. I commend my foremen when I see they
have distributed the best things to the most deserving, but, if I see
that someone is winning special treatment as a result of flattery or
some pointless service, I do not let it pass but rebuke the foreman
and try to show him that his actions are not helpful, not even to
himself.'

XIV

'So now that your foreman has the skill of governing,' I said, 'and can
therefore command obedience, do you consider him perfectly qualified, or does he need anything else, even though he possesses the skills
you have mentioned?'

'Certainly he does,' said Ischomachus. 'He needs to keep his hands 2
off his master's property, and to avoid theft; for, if the man who con-
trols the harvest is brazen enough to make it disappear so as to leave
the operation with no profit, what benefit will you get from his management of your farm?'

'Do you then undertake to teach him this kind of honesty* as well?' 3

'Of course—though I find that not everyone is ready to accept
such instruction. Still, I try to set my slaves on the path to honesty by 4
taking some axioms from Draco's laws and some from Solon's,* as it
seems to me that these men laid down many of their laws with the
teaching of this specific instance of justice* in mind. It is specified, 5

for instance, that theft must be punished, and anyone convicted of it should be imprisoned, and put to death if caught in the act. It is clear that they enacted these laws out of a desire to make greed unprofitable

6 to the wrongdoer. That is why, by adopting some of these laws and borrowing others from those of the Persian King, I try to make my

7 slaves scrupulous in handling my property. The Greek laws simply specify penalties for offenders, whereas the King's* not only punish wrongdoers but also reward the honest. The result is that many people, however acquisitive they may be, see that the honest become richer than the dishonest, and so stay very firmly on the side of

8 upright behaviour. And if I see anyone repeatedly trying to act dishonestly in spite of being well treated, I regard him as incurably greedy and have nothing more to do with him. If, on the other hand,

9 I observe men who are disposed to behave honestly not only because of the advantages this gives them but also because they are anxious for

10 my praise, I treat them as free men,* enriching them and even honouring them as gentlemen. It is this, I think, Socrates, that separates the ambitious man* from the greedy: to be willing, for the sake of praise and good repute, to work hard where necessary, to take risks, and to refrain from dishonest gain.'

XV

'Very well, Ischomachus; when you have instilled in your man a desire for your prosperity, and seen to it that he applies himself to this end; when in addition you have given him the knowledge of how each aspect of his work may yield a bigger surplus; when you have made him qualified to govern others; when, on top of everything, he is as delighted as you would be in producing abundant harvests in due season, I shall no longer ask you if he is short of any further attribute. A man of this kind would, I think, make a very valuable foreman. Do not, however, pass over a point that was only lightly touched on in our discussion.'

2   'And what was that?'

'Well, you did say that the most important lesson to be learnt is how each task should be performed. You said that, unless your man knows what has to be done and how, no good will come of all his diligence.'

At this Ischomachus said, 'Socrates, are you now insisting that 3
I give you a complete course in the art of agriculture?'

'Yes, because this is perhaps the one thing that makes those who
understand it rich, but compels those who don't to live in poverty,
however hard they work.'

'In that case, you will now hear how kindly this art is disposed 4
towards mankind. It is the most useful and most agreeable art to work
at, the most splendid and most congenial to gods and men, and also
the easiest to learn; so it must surely be something noble. "Noble" is,
as you know, what we call those living creatures that are beautiful,
large, useful, and gentle towards man.'

'But, Ischomachus, I do think I understood well enough what you 5
said about the best way to teach a foreman. I believe I grasped what
you said about making him loyal to you, as well as diligent and able to
govern others, and honest.* But you also said that the man who is 6
going to make a success of applying himself to farming must also
learn what he has to do in each situation, and how and when each job
is to be done. It is this aspect that I think we passed over somewhat
superficially. It's as if you said that anyone who is going to take down 7
dictation and read what he's written must know the alphabet. If I'd
been told this, I would admittedly have understood the need to know
my alphabet, but that would have put me no nearer to actually know- 8
ing it. And so, in this case, I am easily persuaded that anyone who
intends to commit himself successfully to farming must first understand what it is; but this understanding doesn't actually tell me *how* to 9
practise it. If I were to decide here and now to take up farming, I think
I would be like a doctor who does the rounds of visiting his patients
without knowing what does them any good. I don't want to be like
him, so I'd like you to teach me what the actual tasks of a farmer are.'

'Very well, Socrates; but farming is not as arduous to learn as other 10
arts, where the student must inevitably be ground down by study
before he can work at it to earn his living. Rather, there are some jobs
you can learn by observing others at work and some simply by being
told, enough to teach someone else, if you so wish. I also think that
you know a lot about farming without realizing it. It is a fact that prac- 11
titioners of other arts tend to conceal their most important aspects,
whereas with farmers the one who is best at planting takes especial
pleasure in being watched while he does it; and the same is true of the
best sower. If ever you ask him about a job well done, he will quite

12 freely tell you how he did it. And so it seems that farming encourages great generosity of character in those who practise it.'

13   'Well, that is a splendid introduction, and not of a kind to deter a listener's curiosity. So you have all the more reason to explain farming to me, seeing it is so easy to learn. For you it is no disgrace to teach an easy subject, whereas for me it would be far more shameful not to grasp it, especially if it is really useful.'

XVI

'VERY well, Socrates. The first thing I want to clarify is something that people who talk about farming* with great theoretical accuracy but no practical experience claim is very complex, but is in fact not

2 difficult at all: they say that anyone who intends to farm successfully must understand the nature of the soil.'

'Yes, and they're quite right,' I said, 'because the man who doesn't know what the soil is suited to produce can't know, I imagine, what to sow or to plant.'

3   'Yes, but he can work out what the soil can or can't bear simply by looking at the crops and trees on someone else's land. When he has this knowledge, there's no point in fighting the gods, since he's not likely to get a good crop by sowing and planting what he wants rather

4 than what the land takes pleasure in producing and nurturing. If, however, through the idleness of its owners, the ground is unable to reveal its potential, you can often get a truer impression from a neigh-

5 bouring plot of land than from a neighbouring farmer. Even land that is uncultivated will reveal its nature; if it produces healthy wild plants, it can, if properly treated, bear excellent cultivated crops as well. In this way, even those not especially skilled in farming can distinguish between types of soil.'

6   'Well, Ischomachus, I now think I am confident enough not to

7 hold back from farming out of ignorance of the soil's nature. In fact, I am now reminded of what fishermen do: though their business is on the sea, and it's not their way to stop and take a look at the shore or slow their boat down, even so, when they are running past farms and see crops on the land, they are not reluctant to express an opinion about which land is bad and which good, disparaging the one and praising the other. And, in general, I observe that they express the

same kind of judgement about good land as those who know about farming.'

'Well then, Socrates, where would you like me to begin refreshing 8 your memory about farming? I'm sure I shall be talking to someone who already knows a lot about how to go about it already.'

'I think the first thing I should be glad to learn—for that is espe- 9 cially a philosopher's way—is how I might cultivate the land if I want to get maximum yield of barley and wheat from it.'

'You know, I take it, that fallow ground has to be prepared for 10 sowing?'

'Yes, I do.' 11

'Then suppose we start ploughing in winter?'

'But the ground would be muddy then.'

'Well, do you think we should do it in summer?'

'But then it will be hard too for an ox-team to turn it over.' 12

'So it looks as if spring is the time to start the job.'

'Yes, that's probably when the soil breaks up most easily under the plough.'

'And at this time, when the grass is ploughed in, it acts as a fertilizer 13 for the soil; it has not yet scattered its seeds and so won't grow again. I imagine you also know that, if fallow ground is to be good, it must be clear of weeds and comprehensively baked in the sun.'

'Yes, definitely. This must I think be done.'

'And do you think it can be done any better than by turning the 14 earth over as often as possible in the summer?'

'Well, I do know for sure', I said, 'that the best way for weeds to be exposed on the surface and wither in the heat, and for the earth to be baked in the sun, is to turn it over with an ox-team at midday in midsummer.'

'And when preparing fallow ground by digging, it's obvious that 15 soil and weeds should be kept apart?'

'Yes, and the weeds should be spread on the surface to wither and the soil turned over so that its exposed part is baked right through.'

XVII

'So you see, Socrates, that we agree about the treatment of fallow ground.'

'It would appear so.'

'What about the best season for sowing?' said Ischomachus. 'Do you know that this should be the season which all men of former times discovered by experiment, and which everyone today has found out to be the best? When autumn ends, everyone looks up to the god to see when he will soak the earth with rain and allow them to sow.'

'All men certainly know* not to sow in dry ground if they can help it, as it's obvious that those who did so before being directed by the god have had to struggle against many setbacks.'

'So on this point all humankind is agreed?'

'Yes, people tend to think alike about what the god teaches. For example, everyone thinks it's best to wear thick clothing in winter, if they can, and also to make a fire if they have the wood.'

'But as to the matter of sowing,' said Ischomachus, 'whether it is best to do it at the beginning, the middle, or the very end of the season, there are many different opinions.'

'And the god doesn't order the years with strict consistency; one year it may be best to sow early, in another mid-season, and in another very late.'

'So what do you think, Socrates? Is it best to choose one time for sowing and stay with that, whether you have a lot of seed or a little, or to start at the beginning of the season and keep going to the end?'

I said, 'I think it's preferable to sow throughout the whole season; better to have enough food at all times than too much at one time and too little at another.'

'Here you agree with me, Socrates, the student with his teacher; and what is more you even gave your opinion before I did.'

'Does scattering seed involve an elaborate skill?'

'We should definitely consider this as well. I imagine that even you know that seed must be scattered by hand?'

'Oh yes; I have seen it being done.'

'And some men can scatter it evenly, while others can't.'

'So it needs practice, so that, as in lyre-playing, the hand obeys the intention.'

'Quite right. But what if some of the soil is light and some on the heavy side?'

'What do you mean?' I said. 'By light do you mean weak and by heavy strong?'

'That is indeed what I mean; and I'm asking if you would give an equal amount of seed to both, or, if not, which should receive more.'

'I'd say that, the stronger the wine is, the more water should be 9 added to it; and, in the case of portering, the heavier load should be given to the stronger man; and, where people are to be fed, I would call on the richest men to feed the greatest number. Still, tell me if poor land becomes stronger when you put more corn into it—just like with draught animals.'

Ischomachus laughed and said, 'I see you're joking, Socrates. But 10 you do need to be aware that, if, after you have sown your seed in the earth, and it has been richly nourished by rain, you plough it in again as soon as it produces green shoots, it turns into food for the soil and becomes its strength, like manure. If, on the other hand, you allow the soil to bring the seed to maturity and bear a crop, it is difficult for weak land to produce a plentiful yield in the end, just as it's difficult for a weak sow to rear a big litter of strong pigs.'

'Do you mean that weaker land should be sown with less seed?' 11

'I most certainly do, Socrates; and you agree with me, because you said that you think weaker beings should always be given lighter loads.'

'What about the men who hoe, Ischomachus? Why do you assign 12 them to work on the grain?'

'I imagine you know that it rains a lot in winter?'

'Of course.'

'Let us suppose, then, that some of our grain will be awash, and buried under mud, and some roots will be laid bare by the downpour. In addition, you know, rain often causes weeds to spring up amid the grain and choke it.'

'It's quite possible for all this to happen.'

'In which case, do you think the grain needs some help?' 13

'Yes, definitely.'

'Then how do you suppose we can help the area that is covered with mud?'

'By lifting off the soil,' I said.

'And what about the part whose roots are exposed?'

'By heaping earth over it again.'

'And what if weeds spring up and choke the grain and rob it of its 14 nutrient, in the same way that useless drones rob bees of the food they have worked hard to store up?'

'We should certainly cut the weeds, just as we evict drones from the hive.'

15 'So it seems a good idea', he said, 'to send in men to hoe?'

'Yes. I am, however, wondering how effective it is to introduce a good comparison here, because your talk of drones made me much angrier with weeds than when you spoke only of weeds.

XVIII

'STILL,' I said, 'the next thing is probably reaping. Tell me what you can about this.'

'I will—unless it becomes evident that you know as much* about this as I do. You do know that the corn has to be cut?'

'Of course I do.'

'When reaping, would you stand with your back to the wind or facing it?'

'Certainly not facing it! It is hard on both eyes and hands, I think, to reap in the face of stalks and chaff.'

2 'And would you cut near the top or close to the ground?'

'If the stalk is short, I'd cut low down, so as to produce more usable straw; but, if it's tall, I think I'd do best to cut in the middle, so that the threshers and winnowers wouldn't have to work too hard on a pointless task. As for the stubble left in the ground, I reckon that it could be used to bulk out the manure heap, or burned to improve the soil.'

3 'You're caught in the act, you see! You know as much about reaping as I do.'

'Perhaps I do. But now I want to see if I know anything about threshing.'

'Well, you presumably know that men use draught animals to thresh grain.'

4 'Yes,' I said, 'I certainly do; and I know that the term draught animals includes oxen, mules, and horses.'

'Do you think that all these beasts know just one thing, that is how to tread the grain as they're being driven?'

'Yes—what else would they know?'

5 'But whose job is it to see that they tread only the correct amount, as uniformly as possible?'

'Obviously the threshers. By continually turning over the untrod-
den grain and throwing it under the beasts' hooves, they can keep it
level over the threshing floor and finish the job as quickly as possible.'

'So you do know as much as I do about this!'

'And then, Ischomachus, we must go on to clean the corn by win- 6
nowing.'

'Yes. And tell me, Socrates, do you know that, if you start on the
windward side of the threshing floor, the chaff will be blown all over
it?'

'This must happen.'

'And it's likely that some of it will fall on the grain.'

'Yes,' I said; 'it's a long way for the chaff to be carried beyond the 7
grain as far as the empty part of the floor.'

'But what if you start winnowing downwind of the floor?'

'It's obvious that the chaff will fall at once into its proper place.'

'And, when you have cleaned the grain over half of the floor, will 8
you go straight on to winnowing the rest of the chaff while the grain
lies about just as it is, or will you first sweep the cleaned portion into
a very small area near the central pole?'*

'I'll sweep up the cleaned grain first, of course, so that the chaff can
be carried into the empty part of the threshing floor, and I don't have
to winnow the same grain twice.'

'Well, Socrates, this proves that you could teach someone the 9
quickest way to clean grain.'

'I didn't realize I knew how to do it; and for some time I've been
wondering if I also had the knowledge to smelt gold, play the flute,
and paint portraits. No one has ever taught me these arts, any more
than farming, and yet I've observed people working at them in the
same way as I've watched them farming.'

'Didn't I tell you just now that farming is the noblest of arts, in that 10
it is the easiest to learn?'*

'Yes, yes, Ischomachus, I've understood. And it turns out I knew
about sowing too without realizing it.'

XIX

'Now,' I said, 'is the planting of trees also a part of farming?'

'Indeed it is,' said Ischomachus.

'So how is it that I knew about sowing, but not about tree-planting?'

2 'Are you sure you don't?'

'How can I, seeing I have no knowledge of the kind of soil to plant in, or how deep or wide to dig the hole, or how much of the tree to bury, or how it should be positioned in the earth to grow best?'

3 'Come on, then, and learn what you don't know. I assume you have seen the kind of trenches that people dig for plants?'

'Yes, I have, many times.'

'And have you ever seen one more than three feet deep?'

'No, certainly not—never more than two and a half feet.'

4 'Now tell me this: have you ever seen one less than one foot deep?'

'Never—not less than a foot and a half, because, if the plants were set too near the surface, they would be uprooted when people dug round them.'

5 'So you know well enough that the depth people dig to is no more than two and a half feet, and no shallower than one and a half feet.'

'It's obvious. I must have observed this.'

6 'Now, can you distinguish dry from wet soil just by looking at it?'

'Yes; at any rate I would say that the land round Lycabettus* and similar is dry, while the marshy ground round Phalerum* and similar is wet.'

7 'Would you dig a deep hole for your plant,' he said, 'in dry or in wet ground?'

'In dry, of course. If you dig deep in wet ground you will come to water, and you can't plant anything in water.'

'You're right, I think. Once the holes have been dug, have you ever observed when it's best to plant each kind of tree?'

'Certainly.'

8 'Very good. Now you want them to grow as fast as possible, so do you think that, if you laid some well-prepared soil underneath them, the shoots from the cutting would make their way more quickly up to hard ground through soft soil or through unbroken earth?'

'Obviously, they would grow faster through prepared earth than through unprepared.'

9 'So a layer of soil must be spread under the plant?'

'Of course.'

'Do you think the cutting would take root better if planted pointing to the sky, or would you set part of it aslant under the layer of earth you have spread below, like a gamma on its back?'

'The latter, surely, because this way there would be more buds 10
underground. I notice that shoots spring from buds above ground,
and I suppose that the same thing happens below ground. And, if
a lot of shoots form in the earth, I imagine the plant will grow quickly
and become strong.'

'You agree with me, then,' he said, 'on this point as well. And would 11
you pile up the soil around the plant, or stamp it down hard?'

'Naturally, I'd stamp it down. If I didn't, I'm well aware that the
rain would turn the loose earth into mud, so the sun would dry it out
as far as the bottom of the hole, so there would be a danger of the
plants either rotting in water or withering because of the heat at their
roots.'

'So it turns out that, in the matter of planting vines, Socrates, you 12
agree with me in every detail.'

'Should one plant fig trees in the same way?' I said.

'Yes, I believe so, and all other fruit trees too. When you're planting
other trees, what is the point of rejecting a method that works well
with vines?'

'But how should we plant the olive?' 13

'You're testing me again, Socrates—you know perfectly well! You
must have seen that for the olive the hole is dug deeper, since it is very
often planted at the roadside. You'll have seen that all the shoots have
stems attached to them, the plants are all tipped with clay, and that
the upper part of every plant is protected by a covering.'

'Yes, I've seen all that.'

'Well, if you have, what aspect of it don't you understand? Or
perhaps you don't know how to place a piece of pottery on top of
the clay?'

'I really do understand everything you have told me about, 14
Ischomachus. But I am wondering how it happened that, when you
asked the general question a little while ago, whether I knew about
planting, I said "No". I didn't think I had anything to say about how
to do it, but now that you've gone on to ask me in detail you say that
my answers tally with what you—a famously expert farmer—know. 15
Is it that questioning, then, is a kind of teaching? The fact is, I have
just seen through your method of questioning me step by step:
you lead me through what I know, and then mention something
similar to it, and persuade me that I know things that I thought
I didn't.'

16   'Then suppose I were to ask you about money,' said Ischomachus,
'whether it is good or bad; would I be able to persuade you that you
knew how to distinguish legitimate from counterfeit? Or if I asked
you about flute-playing, could I persuade you that you knew how to
play the flute? Or from observing painters, that you knew how to
paint—and similarly with other artists?'

        'Possibly, since you have convinced me that I understand farming,
even though no one has ever taught me that art.'

17   'That's not possible, Socrates. But, as I told you before, farming is
such a humane and gentle art that she quickly makes those who observe
18 and listen well informed about her.* She herself teaches us a great deal
about the best way to employ her. For example, a vine, by climbing up
a nearby tree, teaches us how to support it; while its grape-clusters are
still unripe, it spreads out its leaves and tells us to shade whatever is
19 exposed to the sun during that season; and when it is time for the
grapes to sweeten in the sun, by shedding its leaves it teaches us to
strip it and so help the fruit to ripen. And when in its abundance it
reveals some ripe bunches to us and some still sour, it teaches us to
pick her fruit in the way that men pick figs, as each becomes plump.'

XX

THEN I said, 'So how is it, Ischomachus, that, if the rules of farming
are apparently so easy to learn and all alike know what to do, not
everyone is equally successful at it? Some farmers live in great comfort and have more than they need, while others cannot even make
ends meet, and actually fall into debt?'

2   'I'll tell you, Socrates,' he said. 'It's not knowledge or lack of it on
3   the part of farmers that causes some to prosper and others to live in
want. You're not likely to hear stories going round that such and such
an estate has been ruined because the sower didn't sow his seed evenly,
or because he didn't plant in straight rows; or that another man planted
vines in unsuitable ground through ignorance of the kind of soil that
suits vines, or that another didn't know it's a good idea to work over
fallow land before sowing; or because another didn't know that it's
4   advisable to treat the ground with manure. You are far more likely to
hear that this man is getting no crops from his land because he doesn't
care* if it is sown or manured; or that this man has no wine because

he can't be bothered to plant vines or to make sure that what vines he
has are productive; or that another man has neither oil nor figs because
he takes no trouble, and does nothing to get them. It's this kind of ₅
thing, Socrates, that accounts for one farmer being more prosperous
than another, much more than someone getting a reputation for
inventing an ingenious way of running his business. It's the same with ₆
generals: there are aspects of military affairs in which some are more
successful than others, not by reason of their intelligence but clearly in
the degree of trouble they are prepared to take. There are things that
all generals (and most private citizens) know, but some will put them ₇
into practice while others will not. For example: everyone knows that,
when moving through hostile territory, it is better to march in the formation in which men will fight best, if they have to; but, although they ₈
know this, some do it and some don't. They all know that it's the right
thing to post sentries day and night before the camp, but some make
sure this is done and some don't. Again, it is difficult to find anyone ₉
who doesn't know that, when marching through a narrow defile, it is
better to secure the high ground in advance; but, in this case too, some
can be bothered to do this, and others cannot.

Then again, everyone says that fertilizer is an excellent thing in farm- ₁₀
ing, and they can see that it is generated by a natural process; but,
although they understand exactly how it appears, and that it is easy to
amass it in great quantities, some take the trouble to produce it and some ₁₁
don't. Yet the god above sends rain, and every hollow becomes a pool,
and the earth provides all kinds of weeds that anyone who intends to sow
must clear from his land. If he but throws everything he pulls up into the
water, time itself will turn it into something that pleases the land; for is
there a kind of weed or soil that does not turn into fertilizer in stagnant
water? Everyone knows the treatment soil requires, when it is too wet for ₁₂
sowing or too saline for planting, how it needs trenches to drain it, and
how salinity is rectified by mixing with dry or liquid salt-free substances.
Once again, however, some people apply themselves to these jobs and
some do not. If a person is completely ignorant of what the earth can ₁₃
produce, and cannot see a crop or plant on it, and knows no one who can
tell him the truth about it, surely it is much easier for him, whoever he
is, to put soil to the test than to do the same for a horse, let alone a man?
Nothing that the earth reveals aims at deceit; she simply shows with total
clarity and truth what she can do and what she can't. It seems to me that, ₁₄
by making everything simple to grasp and understand, the land has the

best way of showing up bad and lazy men. It's just not possible, as it is
with other arts, for the lazy to make excuses on grounds of ignorance,
15 because, as everyone knows, the earth responds well to good treatment.
Laziness in farming is clear proof of a defective soul.* No human being
can persuade himself that he can live without life's necessities, and if
a man is unwilling to take up farming and knows no other way of making
money, he plainly means to live by theft, robbery, or begging, or else is
completely incapable of reason.

16   Even when there are a good number of labourers, it makes a great
difference to the profitability or not of a farm whether the person in
charge notices if all his men are busy during working hours or is
indifferent to them. In a gang of ten, one man can easily make a dif-
17 ference by working his full stint, and another can do the same by
knocking off before time. Allowing men to take things easy all day
18 long can mean that only half the whole job is completed. You could
compare it to two men walking along a road; both are young and fit,
but their differing speeds open up a gap of a hundred stades in every
two hundred. One keeps going steadily with his mind on his aim,
while the other's laid-back attitude means he keeps taking breaks by
springs or in shady spots, gazing at the view or seeking out gentle
19 breezes. It is the same with agricultural work: there is a great difference in performance between those who finish their appointed task
and those who don't, who think up excuses for not working and are
20 allowed to get away with it. The difference between working effectively and not paying proper attention to one's job is as great as that
between working and being idle. If men are told to hoe to clear vines
of weeds and yet this results in the weeds being healthier and more
numerous than before, would you not call this an example of laziness?

21   It is considerations like these, then, that ruin estates, more often
than sheer lack of knowledge. For outgoings from an estate remain
constant, but, if the work done is not enough to produce a surplus to
22 set against them, it is no wonder if the result is not profit but loss. But
for those who are able to apply themselves resolutely to farming,
nothing offers a more effective way of making money. This is what my
father practised himself and also taught me. He would never let me
buy a plot that was already cultivated but would advise me to acquire
land that through its owner's negligence or incapacity was unworked
23 and unplanted. He said that tilled land was both expensive and could
not be improved; it did not bring its owner the same kind of pleasure,

he reckoned, whereas every plot of land and herd of beasts that showed steady improvement was a source of the greatest enjoyment. And nothing improves more than land that has progressed from a state of 24 neglect to full productivity. I can tell you, Socrates, that we have in the past increased the value of several farms many times over. This principle is so important, and is so easy to learn, that simply by hearing it from me you know as much as I do, and can go away and teach it to someone else, if you have a mind to. My father did not learn it from anyone, nor 25 did he discover it by hard study, but said it was because of his love of farming and of hard work that he wanted a farm that would give him something to occupy him, and at the same time combine profit with 26 enjoyment. I have to tell you, Socrates, that my father was in my view the greatest farming enthusiast in all Athens.'

On hearing this I asked him, 'Did your father keep all the farms he improved, or did he sell them if he could get a good price?'

'Oh, he sold them, of course; but he immediately bought another in an uncultivated state, because he loved being active.'

'You're telling me, Ischomachus, that your father's natural love of 27 farming was exactly the same as a merchant's love of grain. We all know that these traders are so devoted to grain that they will take ship to anywhere they hear there is a great supply of it; they will cross the Aegean, the Black Sea, or the seas around Sicily; and, when they have 28 got hold of as much as they can, they will bring it back over the sea, even stowing it in the same ship they are sailing in themselves. When they need money, they don't unload the grain simply where they happen to be, but take it where it fetches the highest price and men value it most, and sell it there. Your father's love of farming seems to have been something like this.'

In answer to this Ischomachus said, 'You're joking, Socrates; but 29 I still think that people who sell houses as soon as they have built them and then build more are for all that lovers of building.'

'Yes; and I swear solemnly that I believe you, and that all men by nature love what they think will bring them profit.'*

XXI

'I AM however thinking, Ischomachus, of how well you have shaped your argument to support your theme. You have been proposing that of all the arts farming is the easiest to learn, and I am now completely persuaded by all you have said that this is indeed the case.'

2   'Yes, of course,' said Ischomachus. 'But I have to say to you that, as regards the ability to govern, which is common to every activity,* be it farming, politics, estate management, or warfare, I do agree

3   with you that people differ greatly from each other in intelligence. For example, when a trireme is out on the open sea and its crew have to row hard all day to make landfall, some coxswains can by their words and actions spur men's souls to bend willingly to their task, while others are so lacking in intelligence that it takes them more than twice the time to complete the same passage. The former, coxswain and rowers alike, go ashore covered in sweat and congratulating one another, while the latter arrive without raising a sweat, but

4   hating their captain and hated by him. It's the same with generals. Some make their men unwilling to exert themselves or take risks, reluctant and disinclined to obey except under compulsion, and even proud of defying their commander; these officers produce

5   troops who, if caught up in some shameful incident, have no notion of dishonour. Conversely, when divinely inspired, brave, and knowledgeable officers take command of these same men, they will train them, and often others like them, to feel shame at dishonourable behaviour, to conclude that it is better to obey orders, and to take pride in so doing, and to work with enthusiasm, individually and

6   collectively, when they have to. Just as devotion to toil may grow in an individual, so too in a whole army, if led by good commanders, men welcome opportunities to work hard and also to do something meritorious under the gaze of their officers. When commanders

7   are regarded in this light by their men, it is they, I assure you, who are the strong leaders; certainly not those who have the fittest soldiers, the best javelin-throwers or archers or the best cavalry, the ones who are the first to court danger because they excel in horsemanship or light-armed fighting,* but rather those who can inspire

8   their troops with the belief that they are obliged to follow them through fire and every kind of danger. You would be right to call a leader high-minded when he has many followers who share this attitude; and he whose will many arms are prepared to serve may fairly be said to march "with a strong right arm". He is truly a great man who can achieve great things not by physical strength but by the exercise of his will.

It is the same in private undertakings. Whether the person in 9
charge is a foreman or a manager, he who has the ability to instil in his
workmen enthusiasm, energy, and endurance in their labours is the
one to ensure a good outcome and a healthy surplus. If when their 10
master appears at their place of work, Socrates, the one who has abso-
lute power to punish the idle and reward the industrious, they still do
not make a conspicuous effort, I for my part cannot envy him. But, if
when they see him they are stirred to action and each workman feels
an upsurge of energy, a spirit of rivalry, and an ambition to excel, well,
I would say that such a man has something of a kingly nature about 11
him. And this, it seems to me, is of the greatest importance in every
occupation performed by human beings, including farming. This is
not, of course, to say that it can be learnt after simply seeing it in
action, or at a single hearing; no, what I mean is that the man who
hopes to acquire these powers needs education, must possess a good
natural character, and most importantly should be divinely inspired.*
This ability to secure willing obedience is not, I think, an exclusively 12
human gift, but has an element of the divine in it as well, and is plainly
bestowed only on those truly initiated into the mysteries of self-
mastery.* Whereas to act the tyrant over unwilling subjects is in my
view a fate awarded by the gods to those they think deserve to live like
Tantalus* in Hades, who it is said spends eternity in constant fear of
a second death.'

SYMPOSIUM

I

Now, in the matter of gentlemen,* it seems to me worth recording not only how they conduct themselves in their serious dealings but also at times when they are more relaxed.* I should like to describe the company I was in when I came to this conclusion.*

2 It was the occasion of the horse races at the Greater Panathenaic Games.* Callias,* Hipponicus' son, was the lover* of a boy called Autolycus,* who had just won a victory in the pancratium,* and he had taken him to watch the race. When it was over, he was setting off with Autolycus and the boy's father to his house in Piraeus,* accom-

3 panied by Niceratus;* but, catching sight of a party consisting of Socrates,* Critobulus,* Hermogenes,* Antisthenes,* and Charmides,* Callias told a slave* to stay with Autolycus and the others, and went

4 over by himself to Socrates' group. 'This is a lucky meeting!' he said. 'I'm just about to give a dinner for Autolycus and his father,* and I think the arrangements I've made would seem far more brilliant if my dining room were adorned with men of purified soul such as your-selves than if I were to invite generals and cavalry commanders and ambitious seekers of office.'

5 Socrates replied, 'You're always making fun of us. You look down on us because you've paid a lot of money to Protagoras and Gorgias and Prodicus* and many others for instruction in wisdom, and so you regard us as some kind of amateurs in the matter of philosophy.'

6 'I agree', said Callias, 'that in the past I have concealed from you my ability to hold forth at length on intellectual topics, but if you come to my house now I shall demonstrate to you that I am in fact someone to be taken very seriously.'

7 At first, as might be expected, Socrates' party thanked Callias for his invitation but would not promise to join him at dinner; but, when it became clear that he would be very upset at their turning him down, they did go along with him. And so his guests assembled, some after

8 exercise and a rub-down with oil, and some having bathed as well. Autolycus sat next to his father, while the others reclined as normal.

Now, anyone observing what went on there would have concluded that there is in beauty a kind of regal element, especially when its possessor, as in the case of Autolycus, is also endowed with modesty 9 and self-control.* In the first place, just as in darkness a bright light attracts the eyes of all towards it, so on this occasion his beauty drew everyone's gaze towards him; and secondly, there wasn't a man present whose soul* wasn't moved in some way at the sight. Some fell silent, while others showed it by their body-language. Now, all those who are 10 possessed by one of the gods are, I think, worth looking at; but whereas those affected by other gods tend to have bulging eyes, to make terrifying noises, and to be aggressive in their behaviour, those inspired by modest Eros* have a friendly look in their eyes and a gentle pitch to their voice, and control their gestures in a way appropriate to a freeborn man. Such indeed was the change in Callias' demeanour on this occasion, under the influence of Eros, and he was well worth the attention of those who had been initiated into the rites of that god.

The guests were getting on with their dinner in silence, as if 11 instructed by some superior power, when Philippus the comedian knocked at the door, and told the porter to announce who he was and why he wanted to be admitted. He had arrived, he said, with all the equipment he needed for dining in someone else's house,* and moreover his slave was having a bad time because he had nothing to carry and had had no lunch.

Hearing this Callias said, 'Well, gentlemen, it would be a shame to 12 deny him the benefit of my roof, at the very least; so let's have him in.' As he said this, he glanced at Autolycus, clearly trying to see how he would take the joke. But Philippus stood there at the entrance to the 13 men's quarters where the dinner was taking place and said, 'You all know I'm a comedian. I've come here in the firm belief that it is more amusing to arrive at a dinner unasked than if I'd had an invitation.' 'Take a place, then,' said Callias. 'The fact is, the company here has had its fill of seriousness, as you can see, and is perhaps somewhat short of laughter.'*

As they continued with their meal, Philippus kept trying to say some- 14 thing humorous, doubtless in order to perform the service for which he was usually invited to dinners; but when this produced no laughter he lapsed into an obvious sulk, and when a little later he tried another joke, and no one laughed at this either, he stopped in the middle of eating, covered his head with his cloak, and lay at full stretch on his couch.

15   'What's the matter, Philippus?' said Callias. 'Are you in pain?' He
gave a loud groan and said, 'I certainly am, and it hurts a lot, because
laughter has disappeared from the company of men, and so my occupation's gone. In days gone by the only reason I was invited to dinners
was to entertain the company by making them laugh. But why should
anyone invite me now? I can no more be serious than make myself
immortal; what is more, no one will ask me to a meal in the hope of
a return invitation, because everyone knows that there is no tradition
in my house of even sending out for food.' As he said this, he wiped
16   his nose, and it was obvious from the noises he was making that he was
weeping. So they all tried to comfort him, promising they would
laugh the next time, and urged him to eat; and Critobulus actually let
out a guffaw at his fit of self-pity. When Philippus heard them laughing he uncovered his head and encouraged his soul to be of good
cheer, because there were going to be contributions,* and resumed
eating.

II

WHEN the tables had been cleared away, and the diners had poured
a libation and sung a hymn, a man from Syracuse arrived to provide some entertainment. He had brought with him a skilled girl
piper* and a dancing girl expert in acrobatics,* as well as a very
2   pretty boy, who could play the lyre* and dance very well too. This
Syracusan made his living by showing them off as a curiosity. So
the girl played her pipes and the boy his lyre, and it was agreed that
both offered pleasing entertainment. Socrates said, 'My word,
Callias, you've given us a perfect treat; you have not only provided
3   a superb dinner, but also presented us with the most delightful
sights and sounds.' Callias replied, 'We could have some perfume
brought in as well, and that way we could dine surrounded by
pleasant odours.'
        'No, no!' said Socrates. 'Just as clothes of one kind look attractive
on a woman and another on a man, so the smells that suit men and
women are different. You surely can't think that any man smears
himself with scent for the sake of another man. And as for women,
especially young brides like the wives of Niceratus and Critobulus
4   here—what need do they have of extra scent? Their natural perfume

is enough. To women, the smell of the olive oil we use in the gymnasium is more attractive than perfume, and they miss it when they can't smell it. The truth about scent is that, once a man has daubed it on himself, everyone smells the same, whether slave or free; but the smells that arise from freeborn exertions demand an honourable and lengthy regimen of exercise if they are going to give off the genuinely sweet odour of freedom.'

Lycon* said, 'That's all very well for young men; but what should we who no longer frequent the gymnasium smell of?'

'Why, oil of gentlemanliness* of course,' said Socrates.

'And where can you get this oil?'

'Well, certainly not from a perfume-seller.'

'Where then?'

Theognis said:

From good men learn good ways; but bad
Company will spoil even the sense you had.

'Do you hear that, son?' said Lycon.   5

'Of course he does,' said Socrates, 'and he puts it into practice too. At any rate, when he set his heart on winning the pancratium,* with your help he looked around <for those who excel in that event>* and so he will now attach himself to whoever he believes is best qualified to tutor him in gentlemanliness.'

At this several people spoke up. One said, 'Where can I find some-   6 one to instruct me in this?' Another maintained it couldn't be taught, and a third said that, if anything could be learnt, this could.

'Since there's disagreement on this question,' said Socrates, 'let's   7 put it off to another occasion, and deal with the matter at hand; I can see that the dancing girl here has taken up her position, and that someone is bringing in some hoops for her.' The other girl now began   8 to play her flute, and someone standing next to the dancer kept handing her the hoops until she had twelve. Dancing all the while, she threw these spinning up into the air, calculating how high to send them so as to catch them again in a regular sequence.

At this Socrates said, 'This girl's performance, gentlemen, is but   9 one of many proofs that women's natural abilities* are actually in no way inferior to men's, except as regards lack of judgement and physical strength.* So anyone here who has a wife may confidently teach her whatever he would like her to know.'

10   'If that's your opinion, Socrates,' said Antisthenes, 'how is it that you don't personally tutor Xanthippe, instead of living with a wife who is the most difficult of women alive now, and, I believe, of all who ever were or will be?'

'Because', he said, 'I have observed that those who wish to become expert horsemen choose not the most docile horses but the most high-spirited, since they consider that if they can control them they can easily handle any other. So it is with me; because it is my desire to live among and associate with my fellow men, I have got myself this wife, in the sure knowledge that, if I can put up with her, I shall have no difficulty in getting along with the rest of humankind.'*

This account was thought to be not wide of the mark.

11   After this, a circular frame was brought in, to which several knives were fastened, pointing upwards. Over these and back again the dancing girl turned somersaults, much to the onlookers' anxiety, as they thought she might injure herself; but she finished her performance with confidence, and suffered no harm.

12   Socrates called across to Antisthenes, 'I don't think anyone watching this would persist in denying that courage too is something that can be taught, when this girl, despite being female, launches herself so boldly at the knives.'

13   Antisthenes replied, 'Would it not then be a very good idea for this Syracusan to exhibit his dancing girl in the city and advertise that for a fee he will make all Athenians brave enough to charge at enemy spear-points?'

14   'Good idea!' said Philippus. 'I'd certainly like to see that demagogue Peisander* being taught how to turn somersaults over knives. The truth is, he can't bear to look a spear in the face, which means he's not prepared even to enrol for a military campaign.'

15   After this the boy did a dance, and Socrates said, 'Did you see? He's a good-looking boy, but appears even more so while performing his dance moves than when he is motionless.' To which Charmides said, 'It looks to me that you are actually praising his dancing master.'

16   'Quite so,' said Socrates, 'because I also noticed that during his dance no part of his body was idle; his neck, legs, and arms were being exercised at the same time, and this is the kind of dancing that develops bodily suppleness. Speaking for myself,' he said to the Syracusan, 'I should very much like you to teach me these dance moves.'

'And what would you do with them?' he said.

'Why, dance, of course!'

Everyone laughed at this, but Socrates said, with a perfectly serious 17 face, 'Are you laughing at me? Is it because I wish to improve my health through exercise, or to improve the quality of my eating and sleeping? Or is it because I'm attracted by this kind of exercise—not like long-distance runners, who develop their legs at the expense of their shoulders, or the way boxers bulk out their shoulders while leaving their legs thin—but because it's the kind that exercises the whole body equally so that it finishes up properly proportioned? Or are you 18 laughing at me because this way I won't have to find an exercise partner or strip off in public at my advanced age, but will be content with a seven-couch room, exactly as this room was large enough just now for the boy to work up a sweat, and because in winter I'll do my exer- 19 cises indoors, and in very hot times in the shade? Or are you laughing at me because my stomach is bigger than it should be and I want to reduce it to a more modest size? Don't you know that the other day Charmides here caught me dancing early in the morning?'

'You're telling me,' said Charmides. 'At first I was astonished, and feared you were going mad; but when I heard you say much the same kind of thing as you did just now, I went home myself, and though I didn't actually dance (because I've never learnt how to) I did practise some arm exercises; I did know how to do these.'

'Quite so', said Philippus; 'and that is why your legs seem to match 20 your shoulders so evenly in strength; I imagine that, if you were to weigh your lower against your upper parts like loaves of bread, the market inspectors would let you get away without a fine.'

Callias said, 'When you're ready to begin your dancing lessons, Socrates, invite me along, so that I can stand opposite and learn with you.'

'Come on, then,' said Philippus; 'let's get the girl to play for me, 21 and I'll dance as well.'

So he stood up and proceeded to mimic the boy's and girl's dances from beginning to end. First of all, because everyone had observed 22 that the boy's dancing postures served to enhance his beauty, he parodied him by making every movement of his body more comical than it naturally was; and, because the girl had bent over backwards to imitate a hoop shape, he tried to do the same, only by bending forward. Finally, since the others had applauded the boy for exercising his whole body in the dance, he told the flute-girl to increase the

tempo and flung himself about, shaking his legs, arms, and head all at
23 the same time. When he had exhausted himself, he lay down on his
couch and said, 'Here is proof, gentlemen, that my kind of dancing
also provides good exercise! It's certainly made me thirsty—so I'd
like the slave to fill that big bowl for me.'

'Let him do it for us, too,' said Callias. 'Laughing at you has made
us thirsty as well.'

24 Here Socrates cut in and said, 'Well, gentlemen, as to drinking, I'm
all for it too. It is a truth that wine irrigates the soul and soothes our
troubles to sleep, in the way that mandragora soothes us, and it also
awakens feelings of good fellowship, just as oil feeds a flame. But it's
25 my opinion that men's bodies behave in the same way as plants growing in the ground: when the god gives them far too much to drink,
they are unable to stand upright or let the air blow through them, but
when they drink only as much as they can enjoy, they stand up tall and
26 flourish and grow to fruition. So it is with us: if we pour ourselves far
too much to drink, our minds and bodies will very soon start to totter,
and we won't be able even to draw breath, still less to say anything
sensible. If, however, our slaves sprinkle us with frequent small
cups—to use an expression of Gorgias'—we will not be driven by the
wine into drunkenness but gradually persuaded by it to arrive at
a more playful mood.'

27 Everyone agreed with him; and Philippus added that the wine-
stewards should imitate good charioteers and drive the cups around
at a smarter speed. This they proceeded to do.

III

AFTER this the boy tuned his lyre to the pipes,* and played and sang.
Everyone applauded, and Charmides added, 'Well, gentlemen, it
seems to me that, just as Socrates said about wine, this combination
of the children's beauty and the sound of their singing lulls one's
troubles to sleep and arouses Aphrodite.'*

2 Socrates interposed again, saying, 'These two, we think, clearly
have the ability to give us pleasure, and yet I'm sure we regard ourselves as much better than them. Would it not then be a shameful
thing if we too didn't try, while we're here together, to give each other
some benefit or pleasure?'

At this several people said, 'Very well; you lead off, and tell us how to hold a successful discussion of this kind.'

'In that case,' he said, 'what I would like most would be to pick 3 Callias up on his promise. He said, you recall, that, if we dined with him, he would give us a formal display of his cleverness.'*

'I'll do that,' said Callias, 'but only if you all also bring to the discussion the special talent* that you know you possess.'

'Well,' said Socrates, 'no one is going to object to identifying what he considers his most treasured quality.'

'Very well,' said Callias, 'I shall tell you what I pride myself most 4 on. I believe I have the ability to make men better.'

'How?' said Antisthenes. 'By teaching them a manual trade,* or by teaching them gentlemanliness?'*

'The latter, if gentlemanliness is the same thing as justice.'*

'It certainly is,' said Antisthenes, 'quite indisputably. Courage and cleverness* can, as we know, sometimes seem to be injurious to both one's friends and the city, but justice has absolutely no part in wrongdoing.'

'Right. So, when each one of you has named the benefit* he can 5 offer us, I won't refuse to describe the art that ensures the result that I mentioned. Now it's your turn, Niceratus; tell us the kind of knowledge you pride yourself on.'

'My father', said Niceratus, 'was determined I should develop into a good man, and so he compelled me to learn the complete works of Homer; and even now I could recite the whole of the *Iliad* and *Odyssey* to you from memory.'

'Has it escaped your notice', said Antisthenes, 'that every rhapsode 6 also knows these poems?'

'How could I not, when I listen to them nearly every day?'

'And do you know of any class of people sillier than rhapsodes?'

'Certainly not—not in my view, anyway.'

'It's true,' said Socrates, 'and it's because they obviously don't understand the inner meaning of these poems. You, however, have handed over a great deal of money to Stesimbrotus and Anaximander,* and many others, so you have missed none of their important aspects. But what about you, Critobulus? What do you pride yourself on most?' 7

'On my good looks,'* he said.

'Are you really going to tell us', said Socrates, 'that you are able to make us better by your beauty?'

'If I can't, I shall obviously cut a poor figure.'

8   'And how about you, Antisthenes? What do you pride yourself on?'
'On my wealth,' he said.

Hermogenes asked him if he had a lot of money. 'Not one obol,'* he swore.

'But do you own a lot of land?'

'Probably enough', he said, 'to provide Autolycus here with a dusting down.'*

9   'Well, we shall have to hear from you as well. What about you, Charmides? What do you take particular pride in?'

'The opposite,' he said; 'my poverty.'

'That's a very attractive quality,' said Socrates, 'because it's most unlikely to provoke envy or cause a fight. You don't need a guard to keep it safe, and it grows stronger by neglect.'

10   'Now you, Socrates,' said Callias. 'What do you pride yourself on?'

Socrates screwed his face into a very solemn expression and said, 'Pimping'.*

This made them laugh at him; but he said, 'You may well laugh, but I know that if I wanted to follow this profession I could make a great deal of money.'

11   'And as for you, Philippus,' said Lycon, 'it's obvious you pride yourself on making people laugh.'

'With more reason, I think,' he replied, 'than the actor Callipides,* who gives himself enormous airs because he can reduce huge audiences to tears.'

12   Antisthenes said, 'Won't you also tell us, Lycon, what you take pride in?'

'I will,' he said. 'You must all know that it's in my son here.'

'And he', said someone, 'is clearly proud of having won his prize.'

Autolycus blushed and said, 'Oh no, not at all.'

13   Everyone looked towards him, delighted to hear him speak, and one of them asked, 'What is it then that you are proud of?'

And he said, 'My father', leaning against him as he spoke.

Seeing this, Callias said to Lycon, 'You do realize that you are the richest man in the world?'

'No, I certainly don't.'

'Well, you must know that you wouldn't exchange your son for all the Great King's* riches.'

'I've been caught red-handed!' said Lycon. 'It does look as if I'm the wealthiest man in the world.'

'Now, how about you, Hermogenes?' said Niceratus.   14

'The excellence and influence of my friends', he said, 'and that even with these qualities they still take an interest in me.'

At this everyone looked in his direction, and several of them asked him at the same time to reveal who these were. And he said he was not unwilling to do so.

IV

AND now Socrates said, 'I imagine it now remains for each of us to demonstrate how substantial his claim is.'

'You might like to listen to me first,' said Callias. 'My point is that all the time I'm listening to you all being perplexed as to the nature of justice* I am actually making people more just.'

'Very clever,' said Socrates. 'And how do you do that?'

'By giving them money, of course.'

At this Antisthenes rose to his feet and began to interrogate him 2 aggressively, as if they were in court. 'Callias, where do you think people keep their justice—in their souls* or in their wallets?'

'In their souls.'

'So you make their souls more just by putting money in their wallets?'

'Of course.'

'How?'

'Because, when they know they can pay for life's essentials, they won't be tempted to risk committing crimes.'

'And do they actually pay back what they get from you?'   3

'Dear me, no—far from it.'

'Well, do they thank you instead of paying up?'

'Absolutely not that either. In fact, some of them behave even worse towards me than before they got their hands on my money.'

'It is indeed extraordinary',* said Antisthenes, staring at him like someone cross-examining, 'that you can make them behave justly toward others but not to yourself.'

'What is extraordinary about that?' said Callias. 'You must have 4 seen plenty of carpenters and builders who construct houses for many other people but can't do it for themselves, and so live in rented accommodation. You have to admit you're defeated, my quibbling* friend.'

5   'He certainly should,' said Socrates. 'Even seers, as we know, are supposed to foretell the future for others but are incapable of seeing what is coming their own way.'

Here this discussion came to an end.

6   Niceratus was the next to speak: 'You may like to hear my view as well, which is that keeping company with me will make you better people. You know, of course, that the great sage Homer has pronounced on just about everything that concerns mankind. So, if any one of you wishes to become an expert in estate management or political speaking or military tactics, or to become like Achilles or Ajax or Nestor or Odysseus, he should cultivate me, because I understand all this.'

'Oh yes?' said Antisthenes. 'Do you also understand kingship, simply because you know that Homer praises Agamemnon for being "a good king and a mighty spearman"?'*

'Of course I do,' he said; 'I also know that when driving a chariot you have to keep close to the turning post:

And lean a little way yourself to the left in your well-woven
chariot-body, whipping on and calling out to your
right-hand horse, giving it free rein with your hands.*

7   'There is something else I know, which you can test here and now. Homer says somewhere, "an onion as relish for their drink".* So, if someone will fetch an onion, you will immediately get the benefit of it, because you will enjoy your drinking all the more.'

8   At this Charmides said, 'Gentlemen, Niceratus means to go home smelling of onions, so that his wife will believe that no one has even thought of kissing him.'

'Very true,' said Socrates. 'But we're in danger of looking ridiculous in another way. It does indeed appear that the onion is a relish, since it adds taste to drink as well as food; but if we nibble one after dinner as well as before we must take care that no one says we called on Callias simply to indulge ourselves.'

9   'Oh dear, no, Socrates,' he said. 'It's all right to munch an onion before going into battle, in the way that some people feed their cocks garlic before matching them in a fight. But we are presumably planning to give someone a kiss, not to start a fight.'

This was pretty well how that conversation ended.

Critobulus then said, 'It's my turn, so I'll tell you my reasons for 10 priding myself on my good looks.'

'Say on,' they said.

'Well then; if I am not good looking, as I think I am, you could reasonably be sued for deceit, because without being put on oath you are always saying I am so. What is more, I believe you, as I consider you to be gentlemen.* But if I really am good looking, and your feel- 11 ings for me are the same as mine are for the one I consider beautiful, I swear by all the gods that I would not exchange the Great King's* realm for the gift of beauty. The truth is, I get more pleasure from 12 gazing at Cleinias than at all the other beautiful things in the world, and I would rather be blind to everything else than to Cleinias alone. I get frustrated with night and sleep because then I can't see him, and I'm deeply grateful to the day and the sun because they reveal him to 13 me. And, again, we handsome men are justified in priding ourselves on the fact that, whereas the strong man must work hard to attain success, and the courageous man by running risks, and the clever man of course by talking, the good-looking man can have it all by doing 14 absolutely nothing. In my case at any rate, although I know that money is an agreeable thing to have, I would rather give all I have to Cleinias than acquire more from someone else; and I'd sooner be a slave* than a free man if only Cleinias would consent to be my mas- ter. The fact is, I would find it less trouble to work for him than to do nothing, and it would give me more pleasure to take risks on his behalf than to live without risk.

So if you, Callias, pride yourself on your ability to make men* more 15 just, I have a juster claim than you in that I can lead them to the heights of excellence.* Because we handsome men are a kind of inspiration to our lovers, we make them more generous with money, more steadfast and eager for glory in the face of danger, and indeed more modest and self-disciplined,* because they feel a sense of shame about precisely what they most desire. People who don't choose good-looking men as 16 generals are mad; personally, with Cleinias beside me I'd walk through fire, and I know that all of you would do so with me. So, Socrates, you shouldn't be in any doubt that my good looks can help mankind. 17 Moreover, beauty shouldn't be disdained because it soon passes its prime; just as it can be seen in a boy, so it can in a youth, a mature man, and an old man. Evidence for this is that handsome old men are

chosen to carry the olive shoots for Athena,* which proves that beauty
18 is common to every age. And, if getting people to do what you want of
their own free will gives you pleasure, I'm pretty sure I could right
now, without saying a word, persuade this boy or girl to give me a kiss
19 sooner than you could, Socrates, however lengthy and clever your
arguments.'

'What's this?' said Socrates. 'You boast as if you were actually
better looking than me?'

'I certainly am,' said Critobulus; 'otherwise I'd be the ugliest satyr-
play Silenus* you've seen.'

20 'Very well,' he said. 'When this present conversation has done the
rounds, you must remember to hold a beauty contest; and our judges
should be not Priam's son Alexander but the very ones you think are
keen to kiss you.'

21 'Wouldn't you ask Cleinias to do it, Socrates?'

'Can't you stop thinking about Cleinias?' he said.

'If I don't mention his name, do you suppose I'm thinking less
about him? Don't you realize that I have such a clear image of him in
my soul that if I were a sculptor or painter I would be able to produce
as good a likeness of him as if I were looking at him in the flesh?'

22 Socrates countered, 'In that case, if you have such a lifelike image
of him, why do you make my life a misery by dragging me off to where
you can see him in person?'

'Because, Socrates, the sight of the boy himself can make me happy,
whereas looking at his image, so far from giving pleasure, fills me with
longing.'

23 Hermogenes said, 'I don't think it's at all like you, Socrates, to do
nothing about Critobulus when he's smitten with a passion like this.'

'Do you think he's been in this state only since he's been keeping
company with me?'

'If he hasn't, when did it start?'

'Have you not noticed that the fuzz on Critobulus' face is just
creeping down toward his ears, while on Cleinias it's already moving
up behind? It was when they were going to the same school that he
became inflamed with this powerful passion for Cleinias. His father
24 noticed this, and handed him over to me to see if I could help; and he
really is much better now. Before this he used to stare at Cleinias with
a fixed, stony gaze, the way people look at Gorgons, and he would
25 never leave him alone, but recently I've actually seen him blink. Even

so, it does seem to me, gentlemen—speaking among ourselves—that he has also kissed Cleinias. There is no fiercer way to kindle passion's fires than this; it cannot be satiated, and it fills you with delicious hopes. That is why I say that anyone who hopes to acquire self- 26 control* should avoid the kisses of attractive youngsters.'

Charmides said, 'But look here, Socrates, what do you mean by 27 scaring your friends away from beautiful people like this, when I swear I saw you and Critobulus when you were both at school searching for something in the same book, heads touching and your bare shoulder against his?'

'Oh dear,' said Socrates, 'so that's why my shoulder pained me for 28 more than five days as if I'd been bitten by a wild animal, and I felt something like a sting in my heart. But now, in front of all these witnesses, I give you a public warning not to touch me until you have grown as much hair on your chin as there is on your head.'

This was the kind of mixed teasing and seriousness that went on among them.

Now Callias said, 'It's your turn, Charmides, to tell us why you 29 pride yourself so much on your poverty.'

'Well,' he said, 'it's generally agreed that it is better to be confident than timid, to be free than to be a slave,* to receive attention than to give it to others, and to be trusted rather than distrusted by one's country. To speak for myself, when I was a rich man in this city, in the 30 first place I was always afraid that someone would break into my house and steal my possessions and do me some personal injury. Secondly, I used to cultivate informers, though I knew full well that they were more likely to harm me than I them. On top of this, I was always being ordered by the city to fund some service* or other, and 31 I could never leave town. But now that I have been stripped of my estates abroad,* and can make no profit from my property here, and my household goods have been sold, I can stretch my length and sleep soundly, I enjoy the city's confidence, no one threatens me any more—it's I who threaten others now—and I can go abroad or stay here like any free man. Rich men give up their seats to me and make 32 way for me in the street. Today I am a kind of tyrant, whereas before I was plainly a slave. Then I used to pay my taxes to the people, now the city supports me with the revenue it raises. And another thing: when I was rich people would speak ill of me for associating with Socrates, but now that I'm poor no one is bothered about that any more. Besides, when I had a lot of property, I was forever losing some of it either to the city or due to bad luck, and now I lose nothing because I don't own anything, but live in hope of something coming my way.'

33   'So,' said Callias, 'do you actually pray never to be rich? And if you have a lucky dream do you sacrifice to the powers that avert disaster?'

'I certainly do not,' he said. 'I simply keep going with a kind of recklessness, in the hope of picking up something from somewhere.'

34   'Come on now Antisthenes,' said Socrates, 'it's your turn. Speak up, and tell us why you take such pride in your wealth, meagre though it is.'

'Because, gentlemen, I take the view that it's not in their estates
35   that men's wealth or poverty resides, but in their souls.* I observe that many private citizens who have plenty of money think themselves so poor that they will undergo any hardship or risk to increase it. I know of brothers, too, who have inherited equal shares where one has plenty to live on, and indeed more than enough for his expenses,
36   while the other is short of everything. I know as well of certain tyrants* whose hunger for money leads them to commit more appalling crimes than the most poverty-stricken. It is through want, no doubt, that some people are driven to thieving, others to burglary, and others to slave-dealing; but there are also tyrants who destroy whole
37   households, kill people in vast numbers, and often even sell entire cities into slavery, all for the sake of money. I pity such men profoundly for this very distressing malady, for they seem to me to be in the same predicament as someone who owns plenty and eats plenty yet is never satisfied. As for myself, the total of my possessions is such that I can hardly find them by myself, yet I can eat to the point where I'm no longer hungry and drink until I'm not thirsty. I have enough
38   clothes, so that I feel no colder out of doors than millionaire Callias here, and when I'm in my house I think of my walls as snug tunics and my roof as the thickest of cloaks; and my bedclothes are so comfortable that it's a real job to wake me up. If my body feels the need for sex, I am so content with what is available that any women I approach are more than happy to accommodate me because no one else wants to go
39   near them. All this, then, gives me so much pleasure that I am inclined to pray not to enjoy doing each part of it more, but less, since I sus-
40   pect that some of it gives me more pleasure than is good for me. But

I reckon that the most valuable possession in my wealth is this: that, if someone were to rob me even of what I now own, I can think of no occupation so mean that it would not furnish me with an adequate 41 living. If ever I want to give myself a treat, I don't buy expensive things in the market, since they cost too much, but I go to the larder of my soul.* It makes a great deal of difference to my enjoyment whether I wait to eat or drink until I feel the need, or if I indulge in some lux- 42 ury, like this Thasian wine I'm now drinking, not because I'm thirsty but because it's there. It's certainly true that those who value thriftiness are more likely to be just than people who like spending money, since people who are most content with what they have are least likely 43 to hanker after the possessions of others. It's also worth bearing in mind that this kind of wealth makes people behave like free men. Take Socrates here, from whom I got this wealth: he didn't measure it out by quantity or weight, but simply kept giving me as much as I could carry away. These days I'm not stingy towards any man, but am quite open with all my friends about my affluence and share the wealth of my soul with anyone who wants it. Moreover—and this is the most luxurious 44 of my possessions—I have, as you can see, endless leisure to see what is worth seeing, to listen to what is worth hearing, and—something I value most—the chance to spend the whole day at leisure with Socrates. He too isn't in awe of those who can count out the most gold, but prefers to spend his time with people he finds agreeable.'

That was what Antisthenes said. 'Well,' said Callias, 'I really do 45 envy you your wealth—for many reasons, and particularly because the city doesn't order you about and treat you like a slave, and people don't get angry if you refuse them a loan.'

'Steady on!' said Niceratus. 'Don't go envying him, because I'm hoping to get him to lend me his gift of needing nothing, schooled as I am by Homer to count

> seven tripods untouched by fire, ten talents of gold,
> twenty shining cauldrons, and twelve horses,

by weight and numbers, and so I am forever longing for vast wealth. This may be why some people consider me a touch acquisitive.' At this everyone laughed heartily, thinking he had told the truth.

Someone now said, 'It's up to you, now, Hermogenes, to tell us who 46 your friends are, and show how influential and concerned for your welfare they are, so that your pride in them may appear justified.'

47 'I will. It is perfectly obvious that both Greeks and foreigners believe that the gods know everything about the present and the future. At any rate, all cities and peoples use divination to ask the gods what to do and what not to do. Further, it is also clear that we believe they can do us both good and harm; after all, everyone begs them to
48 avert disasters and grant good fortune. Now, these omniscient and omnipotent gods are so well disposed* towards me that, as a result of their concern, I am never out of their sight by day or night, wherever I am going or whatever I have plans to do. Because of their foreknowledge they also send me messengers about the consequences of any action, in the shape of utterances, dreams, and bird-omens, to tell me what I should or shouldn't do. When I take notice of these, I never regret it, though if ever I've defied them I have been punished.'

49 At this Socrates said, 'There's nothing implausible in what you say. I would, however, like to know what kind of service you do to the gods to keep them so friendly toward you.'

'Of course,' said Hermogenes; 'and it's a very economical one. I praise them, which costs me nothing; I always give them back part of what they give me; I avoid irreligious speech as far as I can; and when I call them to witness in some matter I never knowingly lie.'*

'If this is truly the way you preserve their friendship,'* said Socrates, 'it appears that the gods too appreciate gentlemanliness!'*

This, you see, was the serious way the discussion went.

50 When they got round to Philippus, they asked him what he saw in raising a laugh to make him so proud of himself.

'Should I not feel justified,' he said, 'when I'm known to everyone as a comedian? When people enjoy a bit of good fortune, they're only too glad to give me an invitation to share it, but when they're in trouble, they run from me without a backward glance, afraid of being made to laugh despite themselves.'

51 'You're absolutely right to be proud,' said Niceratus, 'though in my case it's the opposite: with my friends, it's the successful ones who keep out of my way, while those in trouble go on about their family connections with me and never leave me alone.'

52 'I'm sure they do,' said Charmides. Then, turning to the Syracusan, he asked, 'What do you prize yourself on? The boy, I imagine?'

'Absolutely not! I'm desperately afraid on his behalf, because I know that there are people plotting to ruin him.'*

Hearing this, Socrates said, 'Good heavens! What appalling wrong 53
do they think your boy has done them that they want to kill him?'

'No, no,' he said. 'They don't want to kill him, but to persuade him
to sleep with them.'

'And you believe, I imagine, that if this were to happen he would be
ruined?'

'Yes, totally.'

'Don't you sleep with him, then?' 54

'Of course I do, all night and every night.'

'My goodness,' said Socrates, 'you're extraordinarily lucky to have
the kind of skin that means you're unique in not corrupting those you
sleep with. You deserve to pride yourself on that, if on nothing else.'

'But that's not what I pride myself on.' 55

'On what, then?'

'Why, on the idiots who make my living by coming to see my puppets.'

'So that explains', said Philippus, 'why I heard you praying to the
gods the other day that wherever you were they would send you a rich
harvest of grain but a dearth of wits.'

'Very good!' said Callias. 'And now, Socrates, what can you say to 56
support your pride in that dishonourable profession you mentioned?'

'Let us first agree', he said, 'on the function of the pimp.* Do not
hesitate to answer any of my questions, and then we shall know how
far we agree. Is that acceptable?'

'Definitely,' they said; and having once said 'definitely', that is how
they all replied to his remaining questions.

'Do you then think it the function of a good pimp to present his 57
client, male or female, to everyone he meets in an attractive light?'

'Definitely.'

'And one of the ways to ensure this is by a fetching arrangement of
hair and clothes?'

'Definitely.'

'And do we not also know that a person may use the same eyes to 58
express both friendly and hostile looks?'

'Definitely.'

'Again, one may use the same voice to speak both modestly and
aggressively?'

'Definitely.'

'Again, are there not some ways of talking that are offensive, and
others that inspire friendliness?'

'Definitely.'

59 'So the good pimp will teach only those qualities that enhance attractiveness?'

'Definitely.'

'Which would be the better—the pimp who could make people attractive to one person, or to many?'

Here the company divided: some said, 'To a great number, obviously,' while the others simply repeated 'Definitely'.

60 Socrates observed that they were agreed on this point too, and continued, 'If someone could make people attractive to the entire city, wouldn't he be the best pimp of all?'

'Of course he would,' they all replied.

'So, if he could turn his protégés into people like this, he would be justified in priding himself on his occupation, and in charging high fees as well?'

61 Everyone agreed on this point, and Socrates then said, 'Well now, I think Antisthenes here is just that kind of man.'

At this Antisthenes said, 'Are you handing your profession on to me, then?'

'I certainly am,' said Socrates, 'because I can see that you have become an expert in the profession that follows it.'

'And what is that?'

'Pandering,'* he said.

This made Antisthenes quite angry, and he said, 'How can you possibly know if I have ever been involved in this kind of thing?'

62 'Well,' said Socrates, 'I do know that you acted as pander for Callias here with the sophist Prodicus,* when you saw that one had a passion for philosophy and the other a need for cash. And I know you also did it for Hippias of Elis,* from whom Callias learnt his memory system, as a result of which he has become more amorous than ever because

63 he can't forget any beautiful thing he's seen. And, of course, the other day you excited my interest in a visitor from Heraclea by your admiration for him and then sat him next to me—not that I'm not grateful; he seems a real gentleman* to me. Then there's Aeschylus of Phlius;* didn't your praise of him to me and me to him result in the

64 two of us falling in love and chasing after each like hunting dogs? It's seeing your skill at this that makes me think of you as a good pander.* It seems to me that the man who can identify people who have the ability to be useful* to each other, and can make them desire each other's

company, would also be able to bring about friendship between cities,* to arrange suitable marriages, and to be a very useful possession* for cities, friends, and allies. But when I said you would make a good pander, you took it as an insult and became angry.'

'No, no,' he said, 'I don't feel that way now. If, indeed, I do have that talent, I shall turn out to have a soul loaded with riches.'

This was how that round of the discussion ended.

V

NEXT to speak was Callias: 'Critobulus, are you going to refuse to stand against Socrates in the beauty contest?'

'I'm quite sure he is,' said Socrates, 'because he can probably see that the pimp is favoured by the judges.' 2

'That may well be,' said Critobulus, 'but even so I'm not backing down. So come on, convince me, if you have some clever arguments, that you are better looking than me—only,' he added, 'get someone to bring the lamp closer.'

'Very well,' said Socrates, 'my opening move in this case is to summon you to a preliminary hearing;* so answer my questions.'

'Ask away.'

'Do you consider that beauty* resides in human beings alone, or 3 also in other things?'

'Well, of course I think that beauty can reveal itself in horses and cattle and many inanimate objects. I know, at any rate, that a shield can be beautiful, and a sword, and a spear.'

'How can all these be beautiful when there are no similarities 4 between them?'

'They must all be beautiful if they are well made for the functions for which we possess them, or if they are naturally suited to our needs.'

'Do you know why we need eyes?' 5

'For seeing with, naturally.'

'In that case it's obvious my eyes must be more beautiful than yours.'

'How do you make that out?'

'Because yours look only straight in front of you, while mine, because they bulge, can also see sideways.'

'Do you mean that a crab has better vision than any other living thing?'

'Indeed, I do, because nature has designed it for maximum efficiency.'

6 'All right. But whose nose is more beautiful, yours or mine?'

'Mine, I think, if in fact the gods gave us noses to smell with. Your nostrils look down at the ground, whereas mine are spread wide to receive smells from every direction.'

'But how can you call a snub nose more beautiful than a straight one?'

'Because it doesn't erect a barrier between the eyes, but allows them to look wherever they wish, whereas a high-bridged nose spitefully builds a dividing wall between them.'

7 'On the matter of mouths,' said Critobulus, 'I give way. If mouths were created for biting off food, yours can bite off much more than mine. And you think, don't you, that you have a softer kiss because your lips are thick?'

'According to your argument, my mouth is apparently uglier than a donkey's; but don't you regard it as a proof of my superior beauty that even the Naiads, though goddesses, are mothers to Sileni, who resemble me rather than you?'

8 'I can't argue with you any longer!' said Critobulus. 'Get them to cast their votes,* and then I'll know as soon as possible what fine or punishment I must suffer—only do it in secret, because I'm afraid that the wealth you and Antisthenes possess will prove too much for me.'

9 And so the girl and the boy registered their votes in secret. While this was happening, Socrates made sure that the lamp was brought up to shine on Critobulus, so that the judges shouldn't be misled, and
10 that the victor's prize garland should be not ribbons but kisses. When the votes fell out, they were all for Critobulus; and Socrates said, 'Dear me! It looks, Critobulus, as if your cash isn't the same as Callias'. His makes men more just, while yours, like most money, has the power to corrupt both judge and jury.'

VI

THEN some of them urged Critobulus to take his winner's kisses, while others said he should get the guardian's permission; and there were other witty sallies from the rest. But even then Hermogenes stayed silent, so Socrates called out his name and said, 'Can you tell us, Hermogenes, what intemperance* is?'

'If you're asking me for a definition,' he said, 'I can't give you one; but I can tell you what I think it is.' 2

'Right, tell us what you think,' he said.

'Well, my judgement is this: intemperance is annoying one's companions as a result of overindulgence in wine.'

'Do you realize that you too are annoying us by keeping silent?'

'Even when you're all talking?'

'No, when there's a break in conversation.'

'So you haven't grasped that, while you're talking, there's no room to insert even a hair into the discussion, still less a word?'

Socrates said, 'Callias, could you possibly come to the rescue of 3 someone suffering under cross-examination?'

'I can,' he said. 'Every time the pipes are played, we fall completely silent.'

'So you actually want me', said Hermogenes, 'to converse with you to the pipes' accompaniment, just as Nicestratus the actor used to deliver his verse?'

'Oh yes, please do,' said Socrates. 'I believe that, just as a song 4 sounds sweeter when accompanied by pipes, so your remarks would be in some way sweetened by music, especially if you were to wave your hands to emphasize the words, like the girl-piper.'

'What kind of pipe music', said Callias, 'would suit Antisthenes 5 here when he's winning an argument at a drinking party?'

Antisthenes said, 'For the man on the receiving end, a hiss, I think.'

As this conversation continued, the Syracusan, seeing they were 6 enjoying each other's company instead of paying attention to his displays, remarked with a sneer to Socrates, 'Are you the one they call "The Thinker"?'

'Well, isn't that better', he replied, 'than being known as "The Thoughtless"?'

'Yes it would be, but only if you didn't have a reputation as a thinker 7 about higher things.'*

'Do you know of anything higher than the gods?'

'Of course not; but that's not where people say your interests lie, but in completely useless stuff up there.'*

'Even if that were so, I might still be interested in the gods, since it's from up there that they send rain to help us and from up there that they provide our light. If you find this a dry answer, it's your fault for provoking me.'

8   'Very well,' he said, 'let's not bother with that. Instead, tell me how far away you are from me in fleas' feet.* This is how people say you measure distances.'

At this Antisthenes broke in, 'Now, Philippus, you're clever at making comparisons; does this fellow look to you like someone wanting to swap insults?'

'Definitely,' said Philippus, 'and a lot of others think so too.'

9   'Even so,' said Socrates, 'don't go making comparisons with him, in case you too look as if you're handing out insults.'

'But if I were to compare him to the best of gentlemen, you would be right to liken me to a eulogizer rather than an insulter.'

'But that's just what you look like now if you're saying that everyone is better than him!'*

10   'Well, do you want me to compare him to worse people, then?'

'No, not them either.'

'So to no one at all?'

'Don't compare him to anyone, in any way.'

'But, if I say nothing, I don't know how I can do anything to deserve my dinner.'

'Easily done,' said Socrates. 'Just keep silent about anything you shouldn't mention.'

Thus was this episode of intemperance doused.

VII

AFTER this, some of the others continued to urge Philippus to make his comparisons, while the rest tried to stop him. In the midst of the hubbub Socrates spoke again: 'Since we all want to speak, perhaps now would be a good time to sing together.' And with that he broke

2   into a song. When he had finished, a potter's wheel was brought in for the dancing-girl, for her to perform on.

At this, Socrates said to the Syracusan, 'Perhaps I really am a thinker, as you say. At any rate, I am now wondering how your boy and girl here could take things more easily while at the same time giving us spectators maximum pleasure—which I know is your

intention too. It seems to me that turning somersaults over knives is ₃
a dangerous spectacle, and quite inappropriate at a drinking party.
Writing and reading aloud on a spinning wheel is possibly also
a remarkable feat, but I cannot imagine what pleasure it affords. Nor
indeed is watching the young and beautiful contorting their bodies
and imitating hoops more enjoyable than observing them at ease. ₄
Now, it is true that it is by no means unusual to encounter marvels, if
that is what you want; there is indeed plenty to wonder at right in
front of you, such as why the lamp there gives out light by having
a bright flame while its bronze container, although bright, emits no
light but reflects other things that appear on it. Or how oil, though
liquid itself, intensifies the flame, while water, which is also wet, extin-
guishes fire. Still, even these questions don't stimulate the attention ₅
that wine does. If, however, the youngsters were to dance to an accompaniment by pipes in figures representing the Graces, the Seasons,
and the Nymphs, I think they would find their task easier and the
party would be much more enjoyable.'

'My goodness,' said the Syracusan, 'that's a splendid idea! I'll put
on a spectacle that you will all enjoy.'

VIII

HE went out amid applause, and Socrates now introduced yet
another theme for discussion. 'Would it not be reasonable, gentlemen, in the presence of a great deity, contemporary with the immortal gods but youngest of them in appearance, whose greatness
pervades all things and who is seated in the soul of man—I mean
Love*—to give some thought to him, especially as we are all his
devotees? Speaking for myself, I can't remember a time when I wasn't ₂
in love with someone, and I know Charmides here has had many
admirers,* and has fallen for a good number himself. And Critobulus,
though still an object of desire,* is starting to yearn for others. And
then there's Niceratus, who as I hear is in love with his wife, who ₃
reciprocates his feelings.* As for Hermogenes, whatever gentlemanliness is, we all know that he is wasting away for love of it. Can you
not see how serious his brow is, how steady his gaze, how moderate
his speech, how gentle his voice, and how affable his nature? Though
he is on familiar terms with the most exalted gods, he doesn't look

down on us mortals. Antisthenes, are you the only one not in love with anyone?'

'Good gracious no,' he said. 'I am in fact madly in love with you.'

4   Socrates turned this into a joke, and answered with mock bashfulness, 'Don't bother me with that now; I have other things to do, as you can see.'

5   'You're always doing this kind of thing,' said Antisthenes, 'playing your own pimp;* everyone can see it. Sometimes you refuse to talk to me with the excuse of your divine sign,* and sometimes because you're bound up in some other interest.'

6   'For heaven's sake, Antisthenes,' said Socrates, 'please don't give me a complete beating. The rest of your rough treatment I can put up with and will continue to do so, as your friend, but let's keep your love

7   for me* a secret, especially since it's not for my soul* but for my good looks.

As for you, Callias, turning to you; the whole city—and, I guess, a good many foreigners too*—knows you are in love with* Autolycus.

8   This is because you are both sons of famous fathers, and are also notable people yourselves. So I have always admired your character, and all the more now, when I observe that the object of your love is not someone spoiled by luxury or corrupted by soft living, but is an example to everyone of strength, endurance, manly courage, and self-control.* To be captivated by qualities such as these is a clue to the

9   lover's own character.* Now, whether there is one Aphrodite or two, the Celestial and the Popular,* I do not know, for even Zeus has many titles and yet is regarded as one and the same god; but I do know that each has her own altars, temples, and sacrifices—more relaxed for

10   the Popular, more reverent for the Celestial. You might then suppose that the Popular Aphrodite gives rise to physical love, and the

11   Celestial to love of the soul, friendship, and noble deeds. It is this kind of love, Callias, that I believe possesses you. My evidence for this is the gentlemanliness* of your loved one, and the fact that I see you involving his father in your meetings with him. There is nothing in them that a gentlemanly lover needs to conceal from his beloved's father.'

12   'My goodness,' said Hermogenes, 'there are many reasons to admire you, Socrates, and now even more so, because, in paying Callias a compliment, you are at the same time educating him in how to behave.'

'That is true,' he said; 'and to increase his happiness I want to show him evidence that love of the soul* is stronger than that of the body. 13 We all know that without friendship there is no association worth mentioning.* Friendship in those who admire character is regarded as a pleasant and willed constraint, while many whose desire is simply physical find fault with their loved one's behaviour and come to be 14 repelled by it. And, even if the affection rests on both aspects, the bloom of youth soon passes its prime, as we know, and with its passing affection* too must fade; but, as long as the soul moves towards 15 greater understanding, the more lovable it becomes. Moreover, in the enjoyment of physical beauty there is also a kind of satiety, which means that a person will inevitably feel in the same way for his beloved as eating too much does for food. Affection for the soul, however, because it is pure, is less subject to satiety—though that does not mean, as one might suppose, that it is less graced by Aphrodite's gifts; on the contrary, when we beg the goddess to grant us words and deeds imbued with her charm, our prayers are also quite clearly answered. It needs no further argument to show that a soul blooming in the 16 beauty of free birth,* and with a modest and noble character, and one that from early days displays a combination of leadership and kindliness to its contemporaries, will admire and feel affection for the object of its love; but I shall go on to demonstrate* to you that such a lover will also have his love returned.* Who could dislike someone by 17 whom he knows he himself is regarded as a gentleman,* and who sees that he is more solicitous for his loved one's good than for his own pleasure, and is moreover certain that, whatever happens, this affection will not be diminished, not even if he loses his mind or falls ill and loses his beauty? Must it not follow that where affection is mutual 18 each takes pleasure in the sight of the other, in amicable converse, in trusting and being trusted; in taking thought for each other, in sharing happiness in good times and sadness when misfortune befalls; living in contentment while they are both healthy, but spending far more time together if one or the other falls ill, and being even more concerned for each other when separated than when they are together? Are not all these things signs of Aphrodite's favour? It is, I would say, by behaving in this way that people preserve their passion for and enjoyment of friendship right into old age.*

Why, on the other hand, should a boy return the affection of* 19 a lover who is infatuated only with his body? Because he allocates to

himself what he desires but assigns to the boy the most shameful role possible? Or because in his desire to wring some concession from his favourite he cuts him off from his friends and family? Again, the fact
20 that he uses persuasion rather than force makes him even more abhorrent; he who employs force exposes his own villainy, while he
21 who works through persuasion corrupts his victim's soul. And why should someone who trades his youth for money love his buyer any more than a market tradesman loves his customer? He certainly won't, as someone in his prime, feel affection for someone past it, or as a handsome youth for someone whose looks have faded, or for an amorous man when he is himself untouched by passion. For boys do
22 not share in the pleasure of sex with a man as women do,* but remain sober while observing the intoxicated passion of someone else. It is not surprising if this breeds in a boy contempt for his lover. Careful investigation would show that when people love each other for their character no serious harm results, whereas shameless intercourse very often leads to generally depraved behaviour.
23   I shall now demonstrate to you how the companionship of a man who takes pleasure in the body rather than the soul lacks the quality of freedom. He who trains another in appropriate speech and behaviour will deserve the honour shown by Achilles to Cheiron and Phoenix;* but the man who lusts only for someone's body may rea-
24 sonably be treated like a beggar, because he is forever following his beloved around, begging and imploring the chance of another kiss or caress. Don't be put off by my somewhat crude words; it's the wine
25 that prompts me, and the love* that is my constant companion which goads me to speak frankly about its rival. In fact, it's my opinion that the man who is interested only in appearance resembles a tenant farmer: his intention is not to increase the farm's value but to produce as large a harvest as he can for himself. He who seeks friendship*
26 however is more like someone owns his farm; at any rate he draws on all the resources he can in order to increase the value of his beloved.* So too with favourites:* the one who knows that by parading his beauty he can easily dominate his lover is most likely to let himself go in other respects, while he who realizes that he cannot keep friendship alive* without also being a gentleman* will probably make more of an
27 effort to pursue excellence.* But the greatest benefit to someone who desires to convert his beloved into a true friend is that he is compelled to practise excellence himself; it is not possible to make your partner

good if you yourself behave badly, nor to encourage self-discipline
and modesty in your beloved if you display shameless or uncontrolled
behaviour.*

   I want to employ myth as well, Callias, to show you that it is not   28
only humankind but also gods and heroes who value friendship of the
soul above physical gratification.* Take Zeus: whenever he fell for   29
mortal women because of their beauty, he allowed them after sex to
retain their mortality, but anyone whose soul* he was enamoured of
he made immortal. Among the latter are Heracles and the Dioscuri,
and there are stories about others too. In my opinion, even in the case   30
of Ganymede, it was not because of his body but his soul* that he was
carried up to Olympus by Zeus. The evidence for this is in his name
(you are of course familiar with Homer):

He rejoices to hear it

which means that he takes pleasure in hearing it. And there is another
place, where

He keeps shrewd schemes in his heart*

This means, "He keeps wise counsel in his heart." So the name of
Ganymede, being made up of these two elements, means that he is
honoured among the gods for the charm of his mind, not his body.
Again, Niceratus, Achilles is portrayed by Homer spectacularly   31
avenging Patroclus' death not as his lover* but as his comrade. So,
too, Orestes and Pylades, and Theseus and Peirithous, and many
other famous demigods, are celebrated in song for performing splendid deeds together not because they slept with each other but out of
mutual admiration.

   Think too of great deeds of our time. Would you not find that they   32
were done to win praise by men who were prepared to undergo hardship and danger rather than by those in the habit of putting pleasure
before good reputation? And yet Pausanias, the lover of the poet
Agathon, actually said in his defence of those who wallow in self-   33
indulgence that the bravest army would be one made up of lovers and
their favourites.* These, he said, would in his view be especially
inhibited by shame* from deserting one another—a very strange
statement, that the people who were most ashamed of doing something
dishonourable should in fact be those in the habit of ignoring criti-   34
cism and treating each other with contempt! He cited as further

evidence the practice of both Thebans and Eleans; he said, at any rate, that though they slept with their favourites they also assigned them the next place to themselves in the battle line. But the example he gives does not hold up, since this practice, though normal among those peoples, is in our view contemptible. In my opinion, stationing their loved ones next to them looks like a lack of confidence in their

35 ability, if left alone, to act as brave men should. The Spartans, on the other hand, who believe that if anyone so much as desires another's body he will never perform a noble deed, train their loved ones to such a pitch of courage that even when deployed among foreigners,* and not stationed in the same rank as their lovers, they are ashamed to

36 desert their comrades. The goddess they revere is not Shamelessness but Shame.* I think we would all agree on the point I am making if we looked at it like this: as between two boys, loved in these different ways, which would you rather trust with your money or your children, or put yourself under an obligation to? For my part, I believe that even the man who is captivated by his loved one's beauty would entrust each of these to the one whose loveliness lies in his soul.

37 In your case, Callias, I think it proper that you should thank the gods for planting a love for Autolycus in you. His desire for honour is quite clear, since he endures a great deal of hardship and pain in order

38 to be proclaimed a victor in the pancratium;* and, if he were resolved not only to confer distinction on himself and his father but also by his manly virtue to be in a position to benefit his friends and to promote his city by setting up trophies over its enemies, and in this way to be marked out and talked about by both Greeks and foreigners*—do you not think he would treat with the greatest respect the person he

39 judged to be his most powerful partner in this whole enterprise? If then you desire his good opinion, you must try to find out what knowledge it was that enabled Themistocles* to liberate Greece, and what kind of knowledge brought Pericles* the fame of being his country's most influential statesman.* You should also examine the wisdom that led Solon* to establish a matchless legal code for the city, and investigate the practices that have bestowed on the Spartans the reputation of being the best military leaders; you are, after all, their proxenos* here, and their most important men always lodge in your

40 house. You must be aware that the city would be quick to entrust itself to you, if you so wished. You have outstanding qualifications for this: you are of noble birth, a descendant of Erechtheus, a priest of the

gods who campaigned with Iacchus against the barbarians,* and in today's festival you are considered to excel your predecessors in the exercise of your office. You possess the most striking physique in the 41 city, and yet are capable of enduring hard labour. If you all think I am talking more seriously than is usual at a drinking party, well, you must not be surprised; for just about all my life I have shared my city's passion for men who combine a noble nature with a keen desire for excellence.'*

The others now began to discuss what he had said, except for 42 Autolycus, who kept his gaze fixed on Callias; who, with a sidelong glance at him, said to Socrates, 'So you're going to act the pimp* between me and the city, to persuade me to enter politics and earn its constant approval?'

'Definitely,' he said, 'if people can see that your commitment to 43 excellence* is not pretended but genuine. False reputation is quickly exposed when put to the test, but true manly virtue, unless marred by some god, brings with it ever more glorious renown when supported by actions.'

IX

THAT is how the discussion came to an end. Autolycus got up to walk home, since it was time for him to go. As his father, Lycon, was leaving with him, he turned and said with feeling, 'Socrates, I regard you as a true gentleman.'*

Next, a chair was brought in, followed by the Syracusan, who said, 2 'Now, gentlemen, Ariadne will enter the bedroom she shares with Dionysus; then Dionysus will come in, having had a few drinks with the gods, and they will have some fun with each other.'

So, first, Ariadne entered dressed as a bride and sat on the chair. 3 Dionysus did not appear yet, but Bacchic music was played on the pipes. Then the dancing master really won their approval, for as soon as Ariadne heard the music her reaction was such that everyone could understand how happy she was to hear it. She did not go to meet Dionysus, or even stand up, but it was plain to see that she could 4 hardly keep still. When Dionysus caught sight of her, he danced over to her, and sinking to his knees embraced and kissed her in the most affectionate way.* Her manner was still modest, but she embraced

5 him lovingly* in return. When the party guests saw this, they kept clapping and shouting 'Encore!' Then Dionysus rose and helped Ariadne to her feet, and they were all able to admire the lovers' acting out kissing and caressing each other. When the party saw that this Dionysus was truly handsome and this Ariadne truly pretty, and that they were not faking but actually kissing with their lips, they were all

6 carried away by the sight, especially as they could hear Dionysus asking her if she loved him and Ariadne swearing that she did; so that not only Dionysus but all those present would have jointly sworn that the boy and girl really were in love with each other, for they gave the impression of not having been rehearsed in their gestures but of

7 being set free to act as they had long desired. At last, when the guests saw them wrapped in each other's arms as if on their way to bed, the bachelors swore they would get married and the married men mounted their horses and rode off to enjoy some wedded bliss.* Socrates and those left behind went out with Callias to join Lycon and his son on their walk.

That is how the drinking party then broke up.

EXPLANATORY NOTES

ESTATE MANAGEMENT

I.1 *I once also heard him*: Xenophon is highly unlikely to have been with Socrates after the battle of Cunaxa; see note on IV.18. Likewise in the opening of *Symposium* (I.1) the narrator claims to have been present at the event involving Socrates that he reports, but in that case we know that Xenophon the author cannot have been; see Introduction, pp. vii–viii, for the essentially fictional character of Socratic dialogue. 'Him' refers to Socrates, for whose connection with Xenophon see Introduction. At *Oec.* 3.1 Socrates makes reference to the friends (*philoi*) who are present and listening to the conversation. Nested within this conversation are the conversations of Cyrus and Lysander (IV.21–5) and Socrates and Ischomachus (VII.1–end) (within which are nested in turn those of Ischomachus and his wife (VII.10–43, VIII.2–10, VIII.17–23, IX.18–19, X.2–8), and a brief exchange between Ischomachus and the helmsman's assistant on a Phoenician merchant ship (VIII.15–16)).

estate management: on estate-management or *oikonomia*, see Introduction, p. x. Xenophon's Socrates views *oikoi* (households) as the building blocks of the *polis* (*Mem.* 3.6.14).

Critobulus: son of Crito, of the deme (village) Alopece (to which Socrates also belonged). A wealthy upper-class Athenian and close associate of Socrates, he was present at the philosopher's trial and death. He appears in other works of Xenophon (including *Symposium*) and in Plato.

branch of knowledge: *epistēmē* (branch of knowledge, science). Plato (*Protagoras* 318e) refers to household management with a synonymous term, *mathēma* (branch of knowledge, science).

I.3 *Socrates*: Socrates of the deme Alopece, son of Sophroniscus I. See Introduction.

I.7 *what is useful*: *ōphelima*, see Glossary (under *ōpheleia*).

rather than wealth: *property . . . wealth*: here and elsewhere in the opening chapters of the work Socrates plays on the closely similar (and rhyming) Greek terms *ktēmata* ('property', 'possession') and *chrēmata* ('wealth', 'property'; also more specifically 'money').

I.8 *how to handle it*: *chrēsthai*: see Glossary, *chraomai*.

I.9 *how to treat them*: *chrēsthai*: see Glossary, *chraomai*.

you consider beneficial things: *ta ōphelounta*, neuter plural participle from *ōpheleō*; see Glossary.

I.10 *flutes*: *auloi* (sing. *aulos*, but the plural may also be used for a single instrument), double-reeded wind instruments.

I.11 *things that benefit us*: ta ōphelounta, neuter plural participle from ōpheleō; see Glossary.

I.13 *concubine*: hetaira ('companion') indicates a prostitute who has fewer clients than (common or garden) pornai and engages in longer-term relationships. The hetairai to which Xenophon refers provided intellectual companionship as well as sex: Aspasia (*Oec.* III.14, *Memorabilia* 2.6.36), Theodote (*Memorabilia* 3.11).

I.14 *what about friends?*: friends (philoi), friendship, and human relationships more generally are a key preoccupation of Xenophon and his Socrates. See Introduction, pp. xxviii–xxx.

I.15 *tyrants*: 'tyrant', Greek tyrannos, describes one who has taken power in a community, not from a hereditary right or through election. The Greeks borrowed the term from Lydia to describe what was a new phenomenon of the archaic period. Originally neutral ('autocrat'), the word gained negative overtones from how the tyrants were remembered negatively. Xenophon's *Hiero* stages a dialogue between a poet and the historical tyrant of Syracuse.

I.17 *a discussion with me about slaves?*: on slaves, see Introduction, n. 1 (p. x) and xii, xvii, xix.

I.20 *profitable activity*: ōphelimōn ergon, helpful/useful works/activities.

I.23 *gentlemen*: kaloi kagathoi, see Glossary.

moderation: sōphrosunē, see Glossary.

souls: psychai (sing. psychē). The soul (psychē) in Homer is the life or breath that leaves the body when one dies, but also a non-animate image of the dead person that lives in Hades. By the fifth century BCE is found the idea of the psychē as the essence of the individual, capable of surviving the body, and also the contrast (especially in the medical writers) between the psychē (as soul or mind) and the sōma (body; pl. sōmata, as here). Socrates regards the psychē as the essence of an individual as a moral being. Note that the word has nothing to do with the Christian concept.

II.1 *I have them pretty well under control*: enkratē, the adjective cognate to the abstract noun enkrateia; see Glossary.

II.3 *five minas*: = 500 drachmas. Socrates would then belong to the class of thetes, those too poor for hoplite service.

II.4 *property is sufficient to answer my needs*: Xenophon's Socrates articulates similar sentiments on the poor as those without sufficient to cover their needs, the rich as those possessing what is sufficient, at *Memorabilia* 2.4.37. For an encomium of poverty, see *Symposium* IV.29–45.

II.5 *guests from abroad*: xenoi (sing. xenos)—guest-friends. The institution of guest-friendship (xenia), fundamental to Greek culture from Homer on, tied together individuals (often of different cities) by hereditary ties of reciprocal hospitality.

II.6 *the city makes many financial demands on you*: the public services demanded of wealthy citizens included covering the expenses of a trireme (maintaining the warship, paying the sailors' wages), of performers in the Athenian dramatic competitions (selection, training, and costuming), or of a team of runners for the festival torch-races (selection, training, other expenses). See VII.3 for reference to how someone required to perform a liturgy could challenge another man he regarded as wealthier to undertake the liturgy instead or exchange property with him.

II.9 *proved me wrong*: *exēlenxas*, lit. 'thoroughly refuted me', submitted me to *elenchos*. The verb recalls the *elenchos* or cross-examination especially characteristic of the Platonic Socrates. Xenophon's Socrates uses the elenchus very selectively, only to make a resistant interlocutor more amenable to his instruction, as at *Memorabilia* 4.2 (the longest elenchus in Xenophon).

and do what I can: *epimeleisthai*—infinitive cognate to the abstract noun *epimeleia*; see Glossary.

to prevent you actually becoming a pauper: on the shift of perspectives characteristic of *Estate Management*, see Introduction, p. xxiii.

II.16 *in all fairness*: *dikaiōs*, lit. 'justly', the adverb cognate with *dikaios*; see Glossary.

III.2 *to themselves and their slaves*: on slaves, see Introduction, n. 1 (p. x) and pp. xii, xvii, xix.

III.4 *the example of slaves*: see note above.

an aspect of estate management that is worth looking into?: in describing estate management as, to translate literally, 'a task/deed/achievement [*ergon*—see Introduction, p. xi] that is worthy of sight', Xenophon employs a term the historians used to indicate the significance of notable deeds. Cf. III.16 (household management compared with achievements in other contexts that are 'worthy of record').

III.7 *performance like the one I mentioned*: Xenophon/Socrates thus elevates this performance (*ergon*—work, deed, achievement) of real life to a status of even more importance than the Athenians' beloved dramatic productions. See also VII.9, where Socrates declares greater interest in the guidance given the housewife than in Games and horse races.

III.10 *useful*: *chrēsimoi*: see Glossary, *chrēsimos*.

results in complete disaster: much of the ensuing work will be devoted to demonstrating women's key role in determining the success or otherwise of an *oikos*. See Introduction, pp. xii-xviii.

III.11 *reasonably be blamed for it*: *dikaiōs*, lit. 'justly', the adverb cognate with *dikaios*; see Glossary.

III.12 *with whom you talk*: the verb *dialegei* ('engage in dialogue') might recall Socratic dialogue. See Introduction, pp. xiii-xix, on this exchange.

III.13 *still very young*: Athenian citizen women ideally married at 13 or 14. See VII.5 and Introduction, p. xiv.

III.14 *Did they train them themselves?*: here we have reflected Xenophon's own interest in training and pedagogy (evident throughout his literary works, including especially the *Education of Cyrus*), and conviction that everyone has the capacity to learn. See Introduction, pp. xx–xxi, xxvii.

I shall introduce Aspasia to you: Aspasia of Miletus, the concubine (*hetaira*: see note on I.13) of Pericles (the most influential Athenian politician of the second half of the fifth century BCE), appears frequently in the works of the Socratics. She is appropriately invoked as an expert, since Socrates' own marriage was notorious (see *Symposium* II.10). Elsewhere too Xenophon and his Socrates confound the usual status categories of women in Classical Athenian ideology. See Introduction, p. xxv. The promise to introduce Aspasia goes unfulfilled in this dialogue and may look ahead to some future occasion.

III.15 *and will explain it all to you*: the Greek verb *epideiknumi* (here *epideixei*, lit. 'she will show you all this'), used here and elsewhere, has connotations of Sophistic display (*epideixis*). On the contemporary sophists, see Introduction, p. xxxii. Socrates and Aspasia sit in intriguing parallel (*epideiknumi* is used also of Socrates, as at 4.1: 'mention', 'point out'), as do Socrates and Theodote, the *hetaira* of *Memorabilia* 3.11.

good partner in the household has as much influence on its prosperity as her husband: on the complementary roles of men and women in contributing to the household, see notes on VII.3–43, IX.1–X.13, and Introduction, pp. xv–xvi.

III.16 *are worthy of record*: see note on III.4.

IV.1 *noblest*: *kallistai*, superlative of *kalon*; see Glossary.

to cultivate: *epimelomenō*, participle of *epimeleomai*; see Glossary.

IV.2 *banausic occupations*: relating to mechanical/technical work (performed indoors, often before a fire, rather than outdoors, like farming). One ancient etymology derives the adjective *banausikos* from the Greek terms for furnace (*baunos*) and kindling a fire (*auein*).

IV.3 *friends or defending their country*: 'city' and 'country' both translate *polis*. Note that friends (*philoi*) along with the city take first place; see note on I.14.

in some cities, especially those with a good reputation in warfare: *polis*, see Glossary. The most obvious examples are Sparta and Persia.

IV.4 *the King of the Persians*: for Xenophon's acquaintance with the Persian Empire, see Introduction, p. x. Xenophon frequently invokes Persia and (see below) Sparta as positive models. His presentation is at times more idealizing than factual. The account of the Persian king anticipates that of Ischomachus and his wife, the king's organization of his empire in several ways sitting in parallel to that of Ischomachus' ideal Athenian *oikos*.

devotes vigorous attention: *epimeleisthai*, see Glossary.

IV.9 *that he cares*: *epimeleisthai*, see Glossary.

IV.16 *Cyrus, that most celebrated King*: Cyrus the Great (Cyrus II), King of Persia 559–530 BCE.

he himself deserved to be: *dikiaōs*, lit. 'justly', the adverb cognate with *dikaios*; see Glossary.

IV.18 *If Cyrus had only lived*: Xenophon segues from Cyrus the Great to Cyrus the Younger, who never reigned, and in 401 BCE was thwarted in his attempt to usurp the throne of his brother Artaxerxes with the assistance of Greek mercenaries, an effort in which Xenophon was personally involved; see Introduction, p. viii. For Xenophon's interest in ideal leadership, see Introduction, p. ix.

a great deal of evidence: Xenophon's historiographical sensibilities inform *Estate Management*, as here, where he employs vocabulary of evidence/proof (*tekmēria* (IV.18: evidence), *mega tekmērion* (IV.19: strong proof)) and reference to sources (IV.18, 19: *legetai*, 'it is said', IV.20: 'told the story to a guest-friend of his').

on his way to fight his brother for the throne: the battle of Cunaxa, 401 BCE. In his *Anabasis* (see Introduction, p. viii), Xenophon describes the battle (1.8, 1.9.30–10.19) and Cyrus' death (1.8.26–7).

IV.19 *obey him willingly*: willing obedience is a crucial plank of Xenophon's conception of ideal leadership.

IV.20 *treated Lysander with great civility*: Spartan admiral responsible for Sparta's victory over Athens in the Peloponnesian War. Xenophon had connections with both Sparta and Persia (see Introduction, pp. viii–ix); and both supply positive models. Xenophon recounts the interactions of Lysander and Cyrus also at *Hellenika* 1.5.1–7, where Lysander negotiates with Cyrus (in 407 BCE) to secure a pay rise for the sailors of the Peloponnesian fleet.

IV.23 *bracelets and other ornaments*: Lysander's assumption that Cyrus' elegant clothes preclude gardening is overturned. Elsewhere too Xenophon underscores that Persian luxury by no means indicates moral or physical weakness (so resisting what was a common Greek attitude, evident, for instance, in Aristophanic comedy and vase painting). At *Anabasis* 1.5.8 he recounts, as an example of excellent discipline, how at the Younger Cyrus' order his nobles—wearing costly and colourful garb—race to pull wagons out of a bog.

IV.25 *I believe you deserve your prosperity*: lit. 'justly [*dikiaōs*, the adverb cognate with *dikaios*; see Glossary] you are *eudaimōn* [happy, blessed, prosperous]'.

your virtue that makes it happen: lit., 'for by being a good [*agathos*] man you are *eudaimōn* [happy]'.

V.1 *for taking it seriously*: Xenophon uses the noun *epimeleia*; see Glossary.

V.5 *his country*: the Greek says *polis*, on which see Glossary.

V.8 *what occupation*: *technē*, see Glossary.

more generous return: lit. 'gives more *charis* [charm, gratitude, favour] in return'. Farming, personified, models human relations. Ideal friendship for Xenophon is fundamentally reciprocal.

welcomes its follower: lit. 'the one attending [*epimelomenon*] to it'; the participle derives from the verb *epimeleomai*; see Glossary.

V.10 *encourages more plentiful festivals*: the description recalls Xenophon's account of his own estate at Scillus in the Peloponnese: *Anabasis* 5.4.7–13.

V.11 *What occupation is more appreciated by slaves, more pleasing to one's wife, more appealing to children*: note the awareness here of the perspectives of slaves, wives, and children. See Introduction, p. xxviii, for a similar phenomenon in *Symposium*.

V.12 *a goddess who teaches justice*: *dikaiosunē*, see Glossary. Xenophon uses farming to further the work's theme of pedagogy. See Introduction, p. xxii–xxiii.

V.16 *more so, indeed, than free men, to make them willing to stay*: slaves are regarded as a part of the system, alongside the leader's other followers, and as capable of demonstrating willing obedience (on which see III.7 and the note on IV.19). For Xenophon's unusual recognition, for his time, of the capacity of slaves, see Introduction, *passim*.

VI.2 *to reach a similar agreement*: for the premium Xenophon's Socrates sets on agreement, see Introduction, p. xxxii.

VI.4 *what is useful*: *ōphelimos*, see Glossary.

VI.6 *and destroy minds*: *psychai*, see Glossary (under *psychē*).

VI.11 *the farmer's life is the finest, the most honourable, and the most agreeable*: lit. finest/most beautiful (*kalliston*), best/most honorable (*ariston*), sweetest/pleasant (*hēdiston*). See Glossary, *kalos*, *agathos*.

VI.12 *we justly term gentlemen*: *kaloi kagathoi*, see Glossary.

VI.14 *respected title of gentleman*: *kaloi kagathoi*, see Glossary; on 'gentlemanliness', see Introduction, pp. xviii–xx, xxiv–xxvi.

VI.17 *Ischomachus*: probably (but not certainly) a historical person, Ischomachus of Athens (deme and parents unknown), alive 460s–c.413 BCE; married to Chrysilla.

in the opinion of women as well as men, foreigners as well as citizens: for Xenophon's tendency to include a variety of perspectives, see Introduction, p. xii.

VII.1 *stoa of Zeus Eleutherios*: built in the last third of the fifth century in the heart of the city of Athens, in the north-west corner of the *agora* (marketplace), which it faced. Designed as a portrait gallery, it housed among other works a painting that illustrated a cavalry battle depicting Xenophon's son Gryllus in the act of killing the Theban general Epaminondas at the battle of Mantinea (362 BCE) (Pausanias 1.3.4, 9.15.5).

agora: marketplace.

VII.2 *arranged to meet some guests*: *xenoi*; see note on II.5.

VII.3 *a property exchange concerning payment for a trireme or a dramatic chorus*: see II.6 on liturgies.

my wife is more than capable: Ischomachus adheres to Athenian protocol: to refer to a citizen woman by name was a breach of etiquette and cast aspersions on her character. She is Chrysilla, with whom Ischomachus had a daughter and two sons. The daughter was given in marriage to a first husband, widowed, then given in marriage for a second time to Callias III (who appears in Xenophon's *Symposium*), who, Andocides reports, slept with her mother, Chrysilla, and then—to the daughter's shame—kept both women (*Andocides* 1.124). Callias went on to marry Chrysilla, probably after Ischomachus' death, and probably because under Athenian inheritance law he could thereby acquire the estate (after making Chrysilla's sons his wards). See Introduction, p. xvii.

managing our domestic affairs on her own: for the agency of his wife as key to Ischomachus' ability to be a gentleman, see Introduction, p. xiv. Only from XI.7 will Ischomachus turn to address other planks of his gentlemanliness.

VII.6 *saw, heard, and spoke as little as possible*: Athenian citizen women were usually secluded within the women's quarters within the house, protected from associating with unrelated males, aside from their participation in occasions connected to the religious sphere (festivals, funerals). See Introduction, p. xiii, for Pericles' advice to Athenian widows that they be the cause of the least talk among men, whether in praise or in blame.

an important discipline in both men and women: lit. 'subject of instruction' (*paideuma*); see Glossary. Here we have a first indication of Ischomachus' tendency to underscore affinities between men and women in fundamental areas of morality.

VII.7 *did you train your wife yourself*: epaideusa, from *paideuō*; see Glossary. On the theme of teaching and learning, see Introduction, p. xx–xxi. (*Didaskō*—teach—occurs frequently too; see note on IX.14.) Xenophon's interest in education is reflected across all his works (as in the *Cyropaedia* or *Education of Cyrus*, and in the didactic treatises).

to carry out her duties: epimeleisthai, infinitive cognate to the abstract noun *epimeleia*; see Glossary.

VII.9 *the most brilliant athletic contest*: kalliston (superlative of *kalon*, for which see Glossary). Socrates regards the real-life example as more interesting than even these events of the Greeks' beloved Games. See also III.7.

VII.10 *tamed and sufficiently domesticated*: women before marriage could be conceptualized by the Greeks as being in a state of wildness associated with nature, in need of domestication. 'Taming' may be applied to animals, but Xenophon commonly employs the same terminology for both people and animals; this need not be pejorative.

to carry on a conversation: dialegesthai. See Introduction, p. xiv.

VII.11 *the best person to take a share in*: lit. 'who would be the best partner/ companion [koinōnos] in'. Here and elsewhere in the work Xenophon's Socrates underscores the notion of marriage as partnership. See Introduction, pp. xiv–xvii.

VII.13 *the more valuable contribution*: 'the better partner' (*koinōnon beltiston*); 'the more valuable contribution' (*ta pleionos axia*—lit. '[contributes] things worthy of more'). Beyond the dowry she brought to the marriage, the wife's contribution turns out to consist in various aspects, not least her capacity to teach other members of the household and increase their value (VII.41).

VII.14 *self-control*: *sōphrosunē* (here and at VII.15); see Glossary. For Ischomachus' remarkable definition of female *sōphrosunē* in VII.15, see Introduction, p. xvi.

VII.16 *fitted you*: lit. 'disposed [you] by nature'; see notes on VII.30 and on *Symposium* II.9.

VII.19 *a most mutually beneficial partnership*: lit., 'in order that the pair may be most useful [*ōphelimōtaton*—superlative deriving from *ōphelimos*; see Glossary] in regard to the partnership [*koinōnia*]'.

VII.22 *work and care*: *erga* and *epimeleia*, see Glossary. Here as elsewhere Xenophon has Ischomachus expose the effort and moral capacity that motherhood demands.

VII.26 *to give and take*: fundamental to Xenophontic ideal human relations and reciprocal friendship (*philia*), on which see Introduction, pp. ix, xxvi, xxviii–xxx.

concern: *epimeleia*, see Glossary.

VII.27 *who has the greater part*: on the depiction here of men's and women's equivalent moral capacity and therefore equivalent capacity for being friends, see Introduction, p. xv.

Self-control too the god has distributed impartially: lit. 'being *enkrateis* ["self-controlled"; the adjective cognate with the all-important virtue of *enkrateia*]'; see Glossary.

VII.30 *naturally more competent*: invoking contemporary debate about the value of *nomos* (law, custom) versus *physis* (nature), Ischomachus presents the law (*nomos*) as endorsing what the god has made men and women capable of by nature (*physis*). Elsewhere too in this section Xenophon employs vocabulary of *physis* ('nature')—e.g., at VII.16, 28.

VII.32 *the queen bee*: on the sustained queen bee metaphor (introduced at VII.17), see Introduction, pp. xiii, xvi–xvii.

the kind of work . . . constantly engrossed in: the Greek uses terminology of *erga* (see Glossary) and *ponos* (labour: *diaponeisthai*, lit. 'to toil constantly') to highlight the queen bee's—and the wife's—toil and achievement through vocabulary that more often describes the deeds of men (and heroes: for example, the Labours (*Ponoi*) of Heracles).

VII.34 *its fair share*: lit. 'what is just', *to dikaion*. The terminology underscores the sense of moral capacity.

VII.36 *gangs of slaves*: on slaves, see Introduction, n. 1 (p. x) and xii, xvii, xix.

VII.36 *while taking thought for*: the Greek (*pronoēteon*, lit. 'thinking in advance') underscores the intellectual process involved in the task. The wife again shows *pronoia* (a 'considerate attitude', lit. 'forethought', 'foresight') at VII.38; the housekeeper at IX.11.

VII.37 *more loyal than before*: on the wife's grasp here of important Xenophontic principles, see Introduction, p. xvii.

VII.42 *if you are seen to be better than me, and can make me your servant*: see p. xvii on Ischomachus' striking observation here about his wife's capacity.

VII.43 *what is good and beautiful*: *ta kala te kagatha* (lit. 'the beautiful and the good things'): neuter plural forms from *kalos* and *agathos*: see Glossary, *kaloi kagathoi*. The goods referred to are both material and spiritual.

　through the exercise of virtues: *tas aretas* (accusative plural, with the definite article *tas*); see Glossary, *aretē* (nominative singular).

VIII.1 *to be more diligent*: lit. 'was moved more towards *epimeleia*'; see Glossary.

VIII.2 *Seeing her distress*: it is his perception of her anxiety that prompts him to the ensuing praise and detailed account of household organization. The level of detail may signal the importance of the topic rather than condescension. See Introduction, pp. xi, xxiii.

VIII.3 *or so satisfactory*: the term used is *kalon*; see Glossary, *kalos*.

　order: *taxis*. Orderliness (by contrast to chaos, *tarachē*: VIII.3, 10) is a theme dear to the heart of Xenophon the soldier (Ischomachus invokes military examples [VIII.4–8]). It surfaces across his works and represents ethical as well as practical accomplishment.

　Take choruses: festivals often featured performance of choruses (people dancing and singing in groups, characteristically in a circular formation); also invoked at VIII.20.

VIII.11 *Phoenician merchant ship*: the analogies from the public sphere generally (cargo ship here, warship [trireme] at VIII.8; choruses at VIII.3; armies at VIII.4–8) have the same effect as those from the Athenian civic sphere (IX.12). See Introduction, p. xv.

VIII.13 *a ten-couch dining room*: this indicates a large dining room; Ischomachus suggests that sailors can fit everything they need into such a space.

VIII.20 *looks like a chorus of objects*: see note on VIII.3. This indicates objects in a circular arrangement.

VIII.23 *the disposition and use of articles*: Ischomachus employs the plural of *skeuē*, a general term that usefully crosses spheres (e.g. of tackle: VIII.11; gear: VIII.12; objects: VIII.22), so underscoring the point that the spheres are parallel.

IX.5 *women's quarters*: wealthier Athenian households had separate quarters for women, often in a more protected part of the house (in an interior room or upper storey), though it is clear in this work that Ischomachus' wife is not confined to those spaces. Literary evidence is clearer than the archaeological on the existence of these areas.

IX.12 *earning a reward*: lit. 'winning honour [*timē*] in return'. It is notable that the housekeeper is imagined to be motivated by the prospect of winning honour (probably especially through praise; see XIV.10)—an exemplary motivation for Xenophon. The wife too can win honour: VII.42.

IX.14 *I explained to her*: lit. 'taught' (from *didaskō*, teach). Here and later the verb (translated in various ways into English) recurs, and points to the importance of teaching and learning in the dialogue. See Introduction, pp. xx-xxi.

IX.15 *just as the Council*: Ischomachus expresses his wife's value through metaphors drawn from the Athenian civic sphere. See Introduction, p. xv.

like a queen: across his works Xenophon draws attention to female leadership in various spheres, including a literal ruler in the case of Mania: *Hellenica* 3.1.10–27.

IX.18 *I was mistaken*: in this paragraph and the next the wife invokes a sustained contrast between care and neglect (employing terms *epimeleisthai* and *amelein*, on which see Glossary) to articulate her opinion that a woman of sound mind (*sōphrōn*) naturally enjoys taking care of what is her own. She displays the important Xenophontic quality of *epimeleia*.

X.1 *your wife thinks like a man*: on this passage, Introduction, p. xvi; see p. xxv for the Socratics' idea that men and women may have the same moral capacity.

instant obedience: the reference is to how quickly the wife learns. Otherwise *Estate Management* downplays the idea of a wife's obedience (see Introduction, p. xvi), despite the fact that the virtue is in other contexts a cardinal one for Xenophon.

Zeuxis: painter from Heraclea in Lucania also mentioned by Xenophon at *Symposium* IV.63 (and *Memorabilia* I.4.3). Here again (as at III.7) Socrates expresses a preference for reality over art, and this segues smoothly into the ensuing discussion of the wife's use of make-up.

X.2 *white powder*: Greek women regularly used cosmetics, including lead-based powders to whiten the complexion, and rouge made from the plant alkanet. The use of make-up could be viewed negatively: see X.13 and Socrates' description of the sophist Prodicus' Vice at *Memorabilia* 2.1.22.

X.5 *how should I seem to be more deserving of your love*: from the early archaic period on, one strand of misogynistic thinking regarded the very mind of woman as different and inferior (e.g. Semonides, *Types of Women* 1). But Ischomachus assumes that his wife's way of looking at things, and her preferences, are much the same as his. He goes so far as to invoke the idea of a 'painted man'—an equivalent to the deceitful, painted first woman, Pandora.

X.7 *alkanet*: see note to X.2.

X.9 *such tricks*: Xenophon has Ischomachus invoke entrenched, misogynistic stereotypes (the idea of women's deceitfulness goes back to Pandora), but then show that she is not essentially or naturally so (she learns to be otherwise).

X.10 *teach others . . . learn anything*: on the theme of teaching and learning, see Introduction, p. xx-xxi.

X.12 *sexually attractive*: remarkably, the husband coaches his wife in how to be more sexually appealing. Athenian ideology sought to suppress female sexuality. More generally, from Homer's Helen and Hesiod's Pandora on, female beauty and sexuality are usually figured as problematic and threatening.

a slave-girl is compelled: on slaves, see Introduction, n. 1 (p. x) and xii, xvii, xix. A slave's body belonged to his or her master.

X.13 *in the way I have taught her*: within the bounds of the dialogue, the teaching of Ischomachus' wife is regarded as completely successful. For the question of whether the later history of Ischomachus' household (if he is the historical individual known from other sources) undermines the picture, see Introduction, pp. xvii-xviii.

XI.1 *about your wife's affairs*: erga, see Glossary and on VII.32; in the following sentence Socrates employs the same term of Ischomachus ('your own business'), again underscoring the parallel between husband and wife. Socrates must prompt Ischomachus to move on to topics other than his exemplary wife, but he will bring her into the conversation again at XI.25.

XI.3 *perfect gentleman*: on 'gentlemanliness', see Introduction, pp. xviii-xx, xxiv-xxvi.

I am known as an idle prattler and an air-measurer: fleetingly recalled is the depiction of Socrates in Aristophanes' *Clouds* (also invoked at *Symp.* VI.6–8); see Introduction, pp. xxxii-xxxiii.

poverty-stricken: see II.4 with note.

XI.4 *Nicias*: not otherwise known.

XI.6 *on a course of excellence*: aretē, see Glossary.

XI.9 *it certainly is*: Ischomachus' reasons for wanting to be rich are pious, philanthropic, and civic in nature: he desires to serve the gods, his friends, and the city. Socrates confirms the honourable character of these motivations (XI.10). Ischomachus stands alongside Socrates as a positive exemplar (see Introduction, pp. xix–xx, xxii, xxiv, for rebuttal of the opposite view), and one who doubtless served as a more realistic and accessible role model for contemporary readers than the philosopher.

XI.13 *by application*: epimelomenōn (lit. 'by taking care'), participle from *epimeleomai*; see Glossary. The verb in various forms, and cognate nouns, are frequently applied to Ischomachus in the ensuing sections (e.g. XI.17: 'I do my best [*epimelomai*] not to lame my horse'; XI.19: 'with schemes [*epimeleiai*] to increase your wealth').

XI.22 *to appear in court*: Athenians represented themselves in court. Rhetoric was a key part of Athenian education, and an essential skill for persuading others in the democracy (in both Assembly and Law Court).

XI.25 *'By my wife'*: on this passage, see Introduction, p. xv.

    making the weaker case appear the stronger: some of the contemporary sophists (see Introduction, p. xxxii) notoriously claimed to do this.

XII.3 *have need of a foreman*: the estates of wealthy Athenians often consisted in several smaller farms rather than a single large plantation, so Ischomachus needs a trusted slave foreman to oversee the other labourers in his absence. (See XII.20 on the importance of the 'master's eye'.)

XII.9 *teach them how to apply themselves*: *epimeleisthai*, see Glossary. It is notable that such qualities as *epimeleia* are regarded as able to be taught and learned (with some qualification (XII.10–14)). For the significance of the theme of teaching and learning, see Introduction, pp. xx-xxi.

XII.17 *explain the training itself*: Ischomachus segues from training people to show *epimeleia*, to the topic of training itself (*to paideuesthai*, see Glossary), a topic of great interest to Xenophon; see note on III.14.

XII.20 *I like the remark attributed to the foreigner*: *barbaros* ('non-Greek, foreigner, barbarian'; Xenophon employs it neutrally rather than pejoratively), frequently used of the Persians, who since the Persian Wars were in Greek eyes the quintessential barbarian.

    I mean when his King had found a good horse: 'the king' is shorthand for 'the Persian king'.

    the best and finest results: *ta kala te k'agatha*, see Glossary.

XIII.5 *fit to be kings*: on the remarkable presentation here of the slave foreman's capacity, see Introduction, p. xix; see also note on XV.4.

XIV.3 *this kind of honesty*: *dikaiosunē*, see Glossary. Ichomachus regards this quality, too (see note on XII.9), as generally teachable.

XIV.4 *Draco's laws and some from Solon's*: Draco (7th c. BCE) and Solon (early 6th c. BCE) were famous Athenian legislators, the latter also a democratic leader, sage, and poet.

XIV.5 *this specific instance of justice*: *dikaiosunē*, see Glossary.

XIV.7 *the King's*: shorthand for the Persian king.

XIV.9 *I treat them as free men*: on this remarkable passage, see Introduction, p. xix.

XIV.10 *the ambitious man*: lit. 'loving honour [*timē*]' (*philotimos*).

XV.6 *loyal . . . diligent and able to govern others, and honest*: Socrates recaps, summarizing Ischomachus' account of how the slave foreman can be taught to be loyal (*eunous*), diligent (*epimelēs*), capable of governing/ruling (*archikos*), and honest/just (*dikaios*)—key qualities of Xenophontic ideal leadership and human relations.

XVI.1 *people who talk about farming*: Ischomachus provides eulogies of the art of agriculture at XV.4, XIX.17.

XVII.2 *All men certainly know*: lit. 'all humans [*anthrōpoi*] know'. The expression is repeated; such knowledge is accessible to all. See Introduction, pp. xx-xxi.

XVIII.1 *unless it becomes evident that you know as much about this as I do*: though not a farmer, Socrates turns out already to know a great deal about farming. See also XVII.2 with note, and XIX.15.

XVIII.8 *will you first sweep the cleaned portion into a very small area near the central pole?*: exactly what Ischomachus is describing is not clear.

XVIII.10 *the noblest of arts, in that it is the easiest to learn*: farming is the noblest art (the adjective suggests high birth) for the very reason of its accessibility to all. See Introduction, pp. xix-xx.

XIX.6 *Lycabettus*: mountain in north-east Athens.

Phalerum: coastal village (deme) of Athens, east of Piraeus.

XIX.17 *well informed about her*: farming (like the land at V.12) is personified as a benevolent female who assists those who want to learn about her.

XX.4 *because he doesn't care*: epimeleisthai (infinitive cognate to the abstract noun *epimeleia*; see Glossary), with a negative, occurs three times in the sentence ('because he doesn't care'; 'because he can't be bothered'; 'because he takes no trouble'), underscoring that a lack of attention, rather than knowledge, more often ruins estates. The importance of the ethical quality of *epimeleia* is further underscored in the ensuing dialogue (as at XX.20: *epimeleisthai*), most vividly at XX.21.

XX.15 *defective soul*: psychē, see Glossary.

XX.29 *will bring them profit*: 'will help them', ōpheleisthai—infinitive cognate to the abstract noun *ōphelia*; see Glossary.

XXI.2 *common to every activity*: on the significance of this remark, see Introduction, p. xii.

XXI.7 *light-armed fighting*: the Greek refers to peltasts, named after their light shield (*peltē*).

XXI.11 *divinely inspired*: for the pious Xenophon, the gods come first and foremost. See also, e.g., V.19, VII.16.

XXI.12 *the mysteries of self-mastery*: sōphrosunē, see Glossary.

Tantalus: mythical wrongdoer punished by Zeus to everlasting thirst and hunger in Hades, though standing in a pool of water beneath a fruit tree.

SYMPOSIUM

I.1 *in the matter of gentlemen*: kaloi kagathoi, see Glossary.

in their serious dealings but also at times when they are more relaxed: for the combination in the work of the playful and serious, see Introduction, pp. xxv-xxvi, xxxi-xxxii.

when I came to this conclusion: Xenophon was too young to have participated in this symposium; on the combination in Socratic dialogue of fact and fiction, see Introduction, pp. vii-viii.

I.2 *the Greater Panathenaic Games*: the festival with athletic games occurred every four years; See Introduction, p. xxxii, for the work's dramatic date of 422 BCE.

Callias: Callias III of the deme Alopece, son of Hipponicus II. Lived *c*.450–367/6 BCE, so still alive at the time Xenophon wrote the dialogue. At his father's death he took his place as the richest man in Greece, but swiftly decimated the family fortune. Half-brother of Hermogenes (I.3). See Introduction, pp. xvii–xviii, for one scandal in which Callias was implicated.

lover of a boy: for the Athenian aristocratic institution of pederasty, see Introduction, p. xxviii.

Autolycus: Autolycus of the deme Thoricus, son of Lycon; executed by The Thirty in 404/3 BCE; see Introduction, pp. xxxiv–xxx.

pancratium: lit. 'all-strength'—a mixture of wrestling and boxing, with no holds barred except for gouging and biting.

Piraeus: one of Athens's harbours.

I.3 *Niceratus*: Niceratus II of the deme Cydantidae, son of Nicias I, a man of great wealth thanks to the family's silver mine holdings.

Socrates: see Introduction, pp. vii–viii, and note on *Estate Management* I.3.

Critobulus: see note on *Estate Management* I.1.

Hermogenes: Hermogenes of the deme Alopece, son of Hipponicus II. Like his half-brother Callias III (see note on I.2), a son of 'the richest man in Greece', but evidently a *nothos* (born outside of a legal marriage), or he would have inherited a share of the paternal estate equal to Callias'. Xenophon in his *Apology* (*Defence of Socrates*) represents Hermogenes as a key source for the end of Socrates' life, and Plato has him present at Socrates' death (*Phaedo*).

Antisthenes: Antisthenes II of Athens, son of Antisthenes I. Lived *c*.446–366 BCE. A disciple of Socrates (whom Xenophon's Socrates claims never leaves his side: *Memorabilia* 3.11.17), present at his death. Antisthenes was also a philosopher and teacher in his own right, and a prolific writer on topics ranging from language and literature, rhetoric and politics, to ethics and epistemology, and in various genres including Socratic dialogue. Only titles and fragments of his writings survive.

Charmides: Charmides of Athens, son of Glaucon III. Lived *c*.446–403 BCE. Appears in several Socratic dialogues, including Xenophon, *Memorabilia* 3.7, and the Platonic dialogue that bears his name (*Charmides*). When he was implicated in the profanation of the Eleusinian Mysteries (415 BCE), his possessions were confiscated and he was sentenced to death *in absentia* (sentences later forgotten, when Alcibiades, also accused, was recalled to the city). Charmides became one of The Ten (Xenophon, *Hellenica* 2.4.19) chosen by the Thirty Tyrants (see Introduction, pp. xxxiv–xxx) to govern the Piraeus. He was killed in the battle of Munychia fighting for The Thirty's forces against the exiled democrats.

I.4 *told a slave*: on slaves, see Introduction, n. 1 (p. x) and xii, xvii, xix.

I.4 *his father*: Autolycus' father Lycon; see note on II.4.

I.5 *Protagoras and Gorgias and Prodicus*: famous sophists. The sophists were itinerant intellectuals of various stripes, many of whom taught rhetoric, an essential skill of those seeking influence in the Athenian democracy. See also Introduction, pp. xxxii, xxxiii.

I.9 *endowed with modesty and self-control*: respectively *aidōs* and *sōphrosunē*, see Glossary.

whose soul wasn't moved: *psychē*, see Glossary.

I.10 *modest Eros*: *erōs*, see Glossary.

I.11 *dining in someone else's house*: in the Greek, the syntax highlights a joke (lit. 'all the equipment he needed—to dine in someone else's house'; his slave 'was having a bad time because he had to carry—nothing').

I.13 *seriousness . . . short of laughter*: for the sustained combination in the work of seriousness and play, see Introduction, pp. xxv-xxvi, xxxi-xxxii.

I.16 *were going to be contributions*: the Greek (*symbolai*) has a pun (= contributions (of food)/hostile encounters).

II.1 *skilled girl piper*: *aulos* player. The *aulos* was a double-reeded wind instrument.

expert in acrobatics: the Greek term (*thaumata*—'acrobatics', 'wonders', 'marvels'; also 'curiosity' (*thauma*) below) initiates what will be a sustained theme of wonders, which may prompt revision of perspectives.

II.2 *play the lyre and dance*: 'lyre' translates *kithara*. The piper, the dancing girl, and this boy are all slaves.

II.4 *Lycon*: Lycon of the deme Thoricus. Lived *c*.470–399 BCE. His son Autolycus was executed by The Thirty in 404/3 BCE, and he joined in Meletus' prosecution of Socrates. See also Introduction, pp. xxxi-xxxii.

oil of gentlemanliness: *kalokagathia*, see Glossary, on 'gentlemanliness', see Introduction, pp. xviii-xx, xxiv-xxvi.

II.5 *winning the pancratium*: see note on I.2.

around <for those who excel in that event>: the words in angled brackets fill a lacuna in the text.

II.9 *women's natural abilities*: *physis*, 'nature'. Unusually for the time (see Introduction, p. xiii), some Socratics (including Antisthenes, the interlocutor who responds to Socrates' remark) believed that virtue was the same in men and women. See Introduction, p. xxv.

except as regards lack of judgement and physical strength: the Greek is ambiguous: *deitai* can mean either 'lacking', or 'deficient in'. See Introduction, p. xxvi, on this passage. The idea that women are deficient in judgement may be intended ironically; across Xenophon's works one finds examples of women demonstrating good judgement.

II.10 *getting along with the rest of humankind*: on this passage, see Introduction, p. xxvii.

II.14 *demagogue Peisander*: a demagogue (from the Greek *demos* ('people') and *agoreuō* ('to speak', especially to the assembly)) is a popular orator; the term is usually disparaging. Peisander of Acharnae, son of Glaucetes, was an Athenian politician and leader in the oligarchic coup of 411 (on which see Introduction, p. xxxiv).

III.1 *to the pipes*: lit. 'to the *aulos*'; see note on II.1.

arouses Aphrodite: the goddess of love, personified desire, who presides over *ta aphrodisia* ('the things of Aphrodite', sex). Socrates will speak of Aphrodite in his long speech in Chapter VIII; see note on VIII.9.

III.3 *of his cleverness*: *sophia*, see Glossary.

the special talent that you know you possess: lit. 'what good thing [*agathon*, see Glossary] you [plural] know about [*epistasthe*, from *epistamai*; see Glossary]'.

III.4 *a manual trade*: *technē* (craft, art, skill) *banausikē*: see note on *Estate Management* IV.2

by teaching them gentlemanliness: *kalokagathia*, see Glossary, on 'gentlemanliness', see Introduction, pp. xviii–xx, xxiv–xxvi.

if gentlemanliness is the same thing as justice: *dikaiosunē*, see glossary; on this passage, see Introduction, p. xxvi.

Courage and cleverness: respectively *andreia* and *sophia*; see Glossary.

III.5 *has named the benefit*: *ōphelimon*, neuter substantive from *ōphelimos*; see Glossary.

III.6 *Stesimbrotus and Anaximander*: Stesimbrotus: a rhapsode from Thasos, mentioned at Plato *Ion* 530d. Anaximander: unknown.

III.7 *my good looks*: *kallos*, see Glossary.

III.8 *'Not one obol'*: an *obolos* was worth one-sixth of a drachma (a drachma being the average daily rate of a skilled worker).

a dusting down: wrestlers would cover themselves with oil, and then sand.

III.10 *'Pimping'*: *mastropeia*, see Glossary.

III.11 *the actor Callippides*: tragic actor, *floruit* fifth century BCE.

III.13 *the Great King*: a moniker for 'the Persian king', on which see note on *Estate Management* IV.4.

IV.1 *justice*: *to dikaion*, substantive from *dikaios*, on which see Glossary.

IV.2 *in their souls*: *psychai* (singular *psychē*), see Glossary.

IV.3 *'it is indeed extraordinary'*: *thaumasta*, 'wondrous' (also 'extraordinary'); sustains the theme of wonders (*thaumaston*, 'wondrous', just below, at IV.4); see note on II.1.

IV.4 *my quibbling friend*: *sophistēs*: sophist (on which see note on I.5 and Introduction, pp. xxxii, xxxiii), quibbler.

IV.6 *mighty spearman*: quotes Homer, *Iliad* 3.179 (as does *Mem.* 3.2.2).

free rein with your hands: quotes Nestor at *Iliad* 23.335–7.

IV.7 *relish for their drink*: quotes *Iliad* 11.630.

IV.11 *I consider you to be gentlemen*: *kaloi kagathoi*, see Glossary.

Great King's realm: see note on III.13.

IV.14 *I'd sooner be a slave*: on slaves, see Introduction, n. 1 (p. x) and xii, xvii, xix.

IV.15 *to make men more just*: the Greek reads *anthrōpoi*, 'human beings'.

heights of excellence: *aretē*, see Glossary.

more modest and self-disciplined: respectively the plural comparative adjective forms of *aidēmōn*—modest, bashful (cognate with *aidōs*, see Glossary)—and *enkratēs*; see Glossary.

IV.17 *olive shoots for Athena*: in the Great Panathenaic festival, on which see note on I.2.

IV.19 *satyr-play Silenus*: Silenus is the companion of Dionysus—god of wine, and of theatre—and father of the satyrs, with whom he appeared in the satyr-play that followed the three tragedies staged by each playwright at the Athenian dramatic festival, the Great Dionysia.

IV.26 *acquire self-control*: *sōphronein* (infinitive of *sōphroneō*, be temperate, self-controlled), cognate with *sōphrosunē*, for which see Glossary.

IV.29 *than to be a slave*: on slaves, see Introduction, n. 1 (p. x) and xii, xvii, xix.

IV.31 *to fund some service or other*: on the liturgies expected of the wealthy, see note on *Estate Management* II.6.

been stripped of my estates abroad: lit. 'beyond [the city's] border'.

IV.35 *in their souls*: *psychai* (singular *psychē*), see Glossary.

IV.36 *certain tyrants*: see note on *Estate Management* I.15.

IV.41 *the larder of my soul*: *psychē*, see Glossary.

IV.48 *so well disposed*: lit. 'friends [*philoi*] to me'. On the importance of friendship to Xenophon, see Introduction, pp. xxviii–xxx.

IV.49 *I never knowingly lie*: on this passage, see Introduction, p. xxx.

you preserve their friendship: lit. 'by being such as this you keep them [as] friends [*philoi*]'.

appreciate gentlemanliness: *kalokagathia*, see Glossary; on 'gentlemanliness', see Introduction, pp. xviii–xx, xxiv–xxvi.

IV.52 *plotting to ruin him*: the passage brings to mind Socrates' trial and one of the charges against him, of ruining/corrupting the young. See Introduction, pp. xxxii–xxxiii.

IV.56 *function of the pimp*: *mastropos*: pimp, procurer; a go-between in clandestine love affairs. See Introduction, pp. xxv–xxvi, xxxi–xxxii, on the sustained mixture of seriousness and levity in this dialogue.

IV.61 *'Pandering'*: *proagōgeia*: lit. 'leading to'; pandering, procuring.

IV.62 *sophist Prodicus*: see note on I.5.

    Hippias of Elis: another of the sophists, on which see I.5 and Introduction, p. xxxiv.

IV.63 *real gentleman*: kaloi kagathoi, see Glossary; on 'gentlemanliness', see Introduction, pp. xviii-xx, xxiv-xxvi.

    Aeschylus of Phlius: unknown.

IV.64 *a good pander*: proagōgos; one who leads on; a pimp, procurer.

    the ability to be useful to each other: ōphelimoi, plural of ōphelimos; see Glossary.

    friendship between cities: lit. 'make cities [*poleis*] friends [*philoi*]'. We see in this passage how the same dynamics of personal relationships apply to those on national (cities) and (in the case of 'allies', below) international levels. For the crucial importance of relationships in Xenophon's thinking, and especially ideal friendship, see Introduction, pp. ix, xvi-xvii, xxvi-xxxi.

    a very useful possession: lit. 'worth a great deal' (*pollou . . . axios*).

V.2 *preliminary hearing*: anakrisis. The way the beauty contest between Socrates and Critobulus is framed in the terminology of a trial in an Athenian law court (also 'case': dikē—lawsuit, trial) adds to other reminders of Socrates' own trial that cast a shadow over the work. See Introduction, pp. xxxi-xxxv.

V.3 *Do you consider that beauty*: to kalon, see kalos in Glossary.

V.8 *Get them to cast their votes*: psēphoi: lit. 'voting pebble', like those used in the Athenian courts. See note on V.2.

VI.1 *what intemperance is*: paroinia: intemperance, drunken behaviour, over-indulgence.

VI.7 *as a thinker about higher things*: on this passage, see Introduction, pp. xxxii-xxxiii. Such 'celestial topics' were in Aristophanes' play *Clouds* presented as a trivial and irrelevant preoccupation of Socrates.

    in completely useless stuff up there: tōn anōphelestatōn—lit. 'the most unhelpful things'—superlative antonym of the adjective Xenophon associates above all with Socrates (ōphelimos, see Glossary). The *an-* is apha-privative (negating the expression), but Socrates' response makes a pun on the preposition *an(a)* 'up' ('from up there', *anōthen*).

VI.8 *how far away you are from me in fleas' feet*: another reference to Aristophanes *Clouds*. See Introduction, pp. xxxii-xxxiii.

VI.9 *everyone is better than him!*: Socrates means that, if Philippus is *comparing* the Syracusan to the best of gentlemen, he implicitly says that he does not belong in the ranks of gentlemen.

VIII.1 *I mean Love*: erōs, see Glossary.

VIII.2 *has had many admirers*: erastai (singular erastēs), see Glossary.

still an object of desire: *erōmenos*, see Glossary.

VIII.3 *who reciprocates his feelings*: *anteratai*, lit. 'feels *erōs* in return'. On this passage, see Introduction, p. xxix.

VIII.5 *playing your own pimp*: lit. 'pimp [*mastropos*] of yourself'.

your divine sign: *daimonion* (lit. 'divine thing'). In Plato's *Apology* (31c–d, 40a) Socrates claims that a *daimonion* in the form of a voice would warn him against taking certain courses of action (including engaging in politics). In Xenophon's *Memorabilia* Socrates recounts how his *daimonion* resisted when he tried to think through his defence speech in advance of the trial (4.8.5).

VIII.7 *your love for me*: *erōs*, see Glossary.

not for my soul: *psychē*, see Glossary.

a good many foreigners too: *xenoi* (singular *xenos*), guest-friends (on which see note on *Estate Management* II.5) or more generally strangers or foreigners.

you are in love with: lit. 'you desire [*erais*: feel *erōs* for]'.

VIII.8 *an example to everyone of strength, endurance, manly courage, and self-control*: respectively *romē*, *karteria*, *andreia* (on which see Glossary), and *sōphrosunē* (on which see Glossary).

VIII.9 *the lover's own character*: lit. 'the *physis* (nature, character) of the *erastēs*' (on which see Glossary).

one Aphrodite or two, the Celestial and the Popular: in Plato's *Symposium*, a guest, Pausanias, invokes the same distinction (180d–181c). On this passage, and desire in the work more generally, see Introduction, pp. xxviii–xxix.

VIII.11 *this is the gentlemanliness*: *kaloi kagathia*, see Glossary; on 'gentlemanliness', see Introduction, pp. xviii–xx, xxiv–xxvi.

VIII.13 *love of the soul*: *erōs* of the *psychē*; see Glossary on both terms.

without friendship . . . worth mentioning: lit. 'without friendship [*philia*], no relationship is worthy of mention [*axiologos*: worthy of speech [*logos*]]'. For the prime importance of relationships and especially friendship in the thinking of Xenophon and his Socrates, see Introduction, pp. ix, xvi–xvii, xxvi–xxxi.

VIII.15 *with its passing affection*: 'affection' here and subsequently (e.g. VIII.15, 17) usually translates Greek *philia*, on which see Glossary.

VIII.16 *in the beauty of free birth*: lit. 'blooming in the beauty of one who is free in character'.

to demonstrate to you: *didaxo* ('I will teach', future form of *didasko*, see Glossary). For the theme of teaching in Xenophon's works, see note on *Estate Management* VII.7.

VIII.17 *love returned*: *antiphileisthai*, 'be an object of love [*philia*] in return'. For the importance of reciprocity in Xenophon's notion of ideal relationships, see Introduction, pp. xv, xix, xxviii–xxix.

regarded as a gentleman: kaloi kagathoi, see Glossary; on 'gentlemanliness', see Introduction, pp. xviii–xx, xxiv–xxvi.

VIII.18 *their passion for and enjoyment of friendship right into old age:* on this striking sentence, see Introduction, p. xxix.

VIII.19 *return the affection of: antiphilēseien,* a 3rd singular optative form of *antiphileō,* 'to feel *philia* [friendship] in return'.

VIII.22 *with a man as women do:* on this passage, see Introduction, p. xxix.

VIII.23 *shown by Achilles to Cheiron and Phoenix:* the centaur Cheiron and Phoenix (for the latter, see Homer, *Iliad* 9) were Achilles' tutors.

VIII.25 *the love that is my constant companion: erōs,* see Glossary. At *Memorabilia* 3.11 Socrates likens his skills to those of the courtesan (*hetaira;* see note on *Estate Management* I.13) Theodote.

who seeks friendship: philia, see Glossary.

VIII.26 *in order to increase the value of his beloved:* lit. 'make his beloved [*erōmenos,* see Glossary] worthy of more [*pleionos axios*]'.

favourites: paidika, see Glossary.

cannot keep friendship alive: philia, see Glossary.

also being a gentleman: kalos kagathos; see Glossary, *kaloi kagathoi.*

VIII.27 *pursue excellence: aretē,* see Glossary.

shameless or uncontrolled behaviour: 'to make your partner good [*agathos,* see Glossary] . . . to encourage self-discipline ["to make your partner *enkratēs*", see Glossary] and modesty [*aidoumenos,* "to have a sense of shame"] . . . if you display shameless or uncontrolled behavior [lit. "if you display *anaischuntia* [shamelessness] and *akrasia* [a lack of control]"].'

VIII.29 *physical gratification:* lit. 'friendship [*philia,* see Glossary] of the soul [*psychē,* see Glossary] above use [*chrēsis*] of the body [*sōma*]'.

anyone whose soul: psychē, see Glossary.

VIII.30 *not because of his body but his soul:* body (*sōma*); soul (*psychē*).

shrewd schemes in his heart: 'He rejoices [*ganutai*] to hear it . . .' 'He keeps shrewd schemes [*mēdea*] in his heart.' The italicized words together approximate to the name Ganymede, *Ganumēdēs.* Neither phrase occurs in our texts of Homer, though expressions similar to the second one are to be found in both *Iliad* and *Odyssey.* Ganymede was the cup-bearer of Zeus.

VIII.31 *not as his lover:* lit. 'not as his boyfriend' (*paidika,* see Glossary). Later authors from the fifth century BCE onwards at times made Achilles and Patroclus lovers, but Homer does not.

VIII.33 *made up of lovers and their favourites:* lit. 'made up of *paidika* and *erastai*', see Glossary. The idea of a brave army made of pairs of lovers occurs in Plato's *Symposium,* but in Phaedrus' speech (178e–179a) rather than Pausanias'. The reference here to Pausanias and Agathon shows that Xenophon knew that work. See Introduction, pp. xxiv, xxviii–xxix.

inhibited by shame from deserting: 'would be ashamed [*aideisthai,* see Glossary] to desert'.

VIII.35 *deployed among foreigners*: xenoi, see note on VIII.7.

VIII.36 *but Shame*: aidōs, see Glossary.

VIII.38 *victor in the pancratium*: see note on I.2.

by both Greeks and foreigners: barbaroi: see note on *Estate Management* XII.20. Here, too, the opinion of foreigners (as well as Greeks) is valued by Socrates.

VIII.39 *Themistocles to liberate Greece*: Themistocles I of the deme Phrearrhi, son of Neocles I. Athenian admiral responsible for the naval victory at Salamis (480 BCE) during the Persian wars.

Pericles: Pericles I of the deme Cholarges, son of Xanthippus I. Lived *c*.495–429 BCE. Influential Athenian democratic politician and general, and brilliant orator. His expansionist and imperialist policies contributed to the outbreak of the Peloponnesian War.

most influential statesman: sumboulos, lit. 'counsellor, wise-advisor'.

Solon: Solon of Athens (early 6th c. BCE): democratic leader, legislator, sage, and poet.

their proxenos: an individual appointed by one state to represent its interests in another.

VIII.40 *with Iacchus against the barbarians*: lit. 'with Iacchus against the *barbaros*' (barbarian/foreigner; frequently used of the Persians, with the singular here indicating their king Xerxes). Iacchus is a name of Dionysus. Herodotus, *Histories* 8.65, recounts the story of how the hymn usually sung to him by pilgrims celebrating the Mysteries at Eleusis came from a divine source during Persian occupation of Athens (480 BCE) and indicated divine assistance coming to the Athenians.

VIII.41 *combine a noble nature with a keen desire for excellence*: the striking sentence (on which see Introduction, p. xxx) culminates Socrates' emphasis on civic benefaction.

VIII.42 *act the pimp*: mastropeuseis: act as *mastropos*, see Glossary.

VIII.43 *commitment to excellence*: aretē, see Glossary.

IX.1 *a true gentleman*: lit. 'a truly exemplary [*kalos kagathos*] person [*anthrōpos*]'.

IX.4 *the most affectionate way*: philikōtata, 'in a most friendly way'.

IX.5 *embraced him lovingly in return*: philikōs, 'in a friendly way'.

IX.7 *some wedded bliss*: see Introduction, p. xxvi, on this surprising end to the symposium.

GLOSSARY

agathos: good, virtuous; substantive *agathon*: good thing, useful/serviceable thing

aideomai: to have a sense of shame, of modesty; to be ashamed (to do something); infinitive *aideisthai*

aidōs: modesty, a sense of shame, self-respect

ameleō (infinitive *amelein*): have no care for, be neglectful of. Antonymous to *epimeleia*

andreia: courage, lit. 'manliness' (from *anēr*, below)

anēr (plural *andres*): a man (opp. to a woman)

anthrōpos (plural *anthrōpoi*): a man, human, mortal (opp. to gods); plural *anthrōpoi*: humankind

aretē: goodness, excellence, virtue

chraomai: use, handle. Xenophon uses the term across all spheres (of humans and animals), without a derogatory undertone

chrēsimos: useful, serviceable (pl. *chrēsimoi*) (adjective cognate with *chraomai*, above)

didaskō: teach, instruct

dikaios: just, fair; *to dikaion*—the just/fair thing

dikaiosunē: justice, righteousness, honesty

dikē: justice

elenchos: cross-examination

enkrateia: self-control, self-mastery; the prerequisite virtue for governing others (according to Xenophon/his Socrates), and the foundation of all other virtue (*Mem.* 1.5.4)

enkratēs: self-controlled, master of (oneself)

epimeleia: attentiveness, care, diligence

epimel(e)omai, infinitive *epimeleisthai*: be attentive to, look after, take care to, cultivate

epimelēs: diligent, attentive

epistamai: know how, know about, understand

erastēs (plural *erastai*): lover. See Introduction p. xxviii

ergon (plural *erga*): work, achievement, deed

erōmenos: beloved. See Introduction p. xxviii

erōs/Erōs: love, lust; the god Eros. See Introduction pp. xxviii–xxx

gunē (plural *gunaikes*): woman, wife

kaloi kagathoi: gentlemen, lit. 'honourable/noble/beautiful and good'; singular *kalos kagathos*; neuter plural *ta kala te kagatha*—lit. '(the) noble/beautiful and good things': refers to material and/or spiritual goods

kallos: beauty

kalokagathia: gentlemanliness, lit. 'nobility/beauty and goodness', exemplarity

kalos: beautiful, noble, good (morally or functionally); the primary reference is to outward form; *to kalon* (neuter form with article)—beauty; the quality of being moral good/functionally excellent

koinōnia: partnership

koinōnos: partner/companion

mastropeia: pimping, pandering (noun)

mastropos: pimp, pander

oikonomia: household/estate management

oikos (plural *oikoi*): estate, household, family

ōpheleō: to help; to be of use, service

ōpheleia: help, assistance; a word Xenophon associates above all with Socrates; adjective *ōphelimos* (neuter plural *ōphelima*): useful, helping, beneficial; the superlative antonym *anōphelestatōn*, lit. 'most unhelpful', appears at *Symp.* VI.7. See Introduction, p. xxxiii

paideuma: thing taught, subject of instruction

paideuō (infinitive *paideuesthai*): train, teach, educate

paidika: boyfriend(s), favourite(s). This neuter plural ('things to do with boys') can designate a single individual

philia: love, friendship, affection

polis (plural *poleis*): city (the city together with the surrounding area: city-state), state

psychē (plural *psychai*): soul, mind. The term has a variety of senses. See note on *Oeconomicus* I.23.

sophia: cleverness, wisdom, intelligence, skill

sōphrōn: of sound mind, sensible

sōphrosunē: moderation, self-control, self-mastery. See Introduction p. xvi

technē: occupation, art, craft

American Literature

British and Irish Literature

Children's Literature

Classics and Ancient Literature

Colonial Literature

Eastern Literature

European Literature

Gothic Literature

History

Medieval Literature

Oxford English Drama

Philosophy

Poetry

Politics

Religion

The Oxford Shakespeare

A complete list of Oxford World's Classics, including Authors in Context, Oxford English Drama, and the Oxford Shakespeare, is available in the UK from the Marketing Services Department, Oxford University Press, Great Clarendon Street, Oxford OX2 6DP, or visit the website at www.oup.com/uk/worldsclassics.

In the USA, visit www.oup.com/us/owc for a complete title list.

Oxford World's Classics are available from all good bookshops. In case of difficulty, customers in the UK should contact Oxford University Press Bookshop, 116 High Street, Oxford OX1 4BR.

A SELECTION OF **OXFORD WORLD'S CLASSICS**